Practising Compassion in Higher Education

Presenting a collective international story, this book demonstrates the importance of compassion as an act of self-care in the face of change and disruption, providing guidance on how to cope under trying conditions in higher education settings.

Practising Compassion in Higher Education presents an opportunity to learn through story and by taking proactive action for our wellbeing. It highlights the need to protect and maintain the wellbeing of staff and students, positioning the COVID-19 pandemic as a major catalyst of disruption. The chapters connect theory with lived experience, exploring self-compassion in work and research, compassion in teaching practice and within the personal/professional blur. The book's contributors bring a range of theoretical and personal perspectives from various global contexts, sharing their own approaches to self-care and how compassion has become a central and crucial element of this practice.

This book takes a unique approach to navigating and surviving the higher education environment and offers valuable lessons for the pandemic era and beyond. This will be an essential resource for students and professionals working in all areas of higher education.

Narelle Lemon is Associate Professor of Education at Swinburne University of Technology, Australia and an internationally recognised researcher in education and initial teacher education bringing an interdisciplinarity across education, arts, and positive psychology. Her particular research expertise and interest relate to fostering wellbeing literacy in K–12 teachers, preservice teachers, and higher degree research students and academics in the higher education sector.

Heidi Harju-Luukkainen is Professor of Education and Vice Director of Kokkola University Consortium Chydenius at the University of Jyväskylä, Finland. She also works as Professor of Education at Nord University, Norway and leads two international research groups and a doctoral program.

Susanne Garvis is Professor of Early Childhood Education at Griffith University, Brisbane, Australia. She is an international expert in policy, quality, and learning with early childhood education and care and has worked in Sweden and Australia. Her work has informed government policy around the world.

Wellbeing and Self-care in Higher Education
Editor: Narelle Lemon

Healthy Relationships in Higher Education
Promoting Wellbeing Across Academia
Edited by Narelle Lemon

Creating a Place for Self-care and Wellbeing in Higher Education
Finding Meaning Across Academia
Edited by Narelle Lemon

Creative Expression and Wellbeing in Higher Education
Making and Movement as Mindful Moments of Self-care
Edited by Narelle Lemon

Reflections on Valuing Wellbeing in Higher Education
Reforming our Acts of Self-care
Edited by Narelle Lemon

Practising Compassion in Higher Education
Caring for Self and Others Through Challenging Times
Edited by Narelle Lemon, Heidi Harju-Luukkainen, and Susanne Garvis

Women Practicing Resilience, Self-care and Wellbeing in Academia
International Stories from Lived Experience
Edited by Ida Fatimawati Adi Badiozaman, Voon Mung Ling and Kiran Sandhu

Supporting and Promoting Staff Wellbeing in Higher Education
A Toolkit for Putting Innovative Practices into Action
Edited by Angela Dobele and Lisa Farrell

Writing Well and Being Well for Your PhD and Beyond
Edited by Katherine Firth

For more information about this series, please visit: www.routledge.com/
Wellbeing-and-Self-care-in-Higher-Education/book-series/WSCHE

Practising Compassion in Higher Education

Caring for Self and Others
Through Challenging Times

Edited by Narelle Lemon,
Heidi Harju-Luukkainen,
and Susanne Garvis

LONDON AND NEW YORK

Designed cover image: © Getty Images

First published 2023
by Routledge
4 Park Square, Milton Park, Abingdon, Oxon OX14 4RN

and by Routledge
605 Third Avenue, New York, NY 10158

Routledge is an imprint of the Taylor & Francis Group, an informa business

© 2023 selection and editorial matter, Narelle Lemon, Heidi Harju-Luukkainen, and Susanne Garvis; individual chapters, the contributors

The right of Narelle Lemon, Heidi Harju-Luukkainen, and Susanne Garvis to be identified as the authors of the editorial material, and of the authors for their individual chapters, has been asserted in accordance with sections 77 and 78 of the Copyright, Designs and Patents Act 1988.

All rights reserved. No part of this book may be reprinted or reproduced or utilised in any form or by any electronic, mechanical, or other means, now known or hereafter invented, including photocopying and recording, or in any information storage or retrieval system, without permission in writing from the publishers.

Trademark notice: Product or corporate names may be trademarks or registered trademarks, and are used only for identification and explanation without intent to infringe.

British Library Cataloguing-in-Publication Data
A catalogue record for this book is available from the British Library

Library of Congress Cataloging-in-Publication Data
Names: Lemon, Narelle, editor. | Harju-Luukkainen, Heidi, 1977– editor. |
    Garvis, Susanne, editor.
Title: Practising compassion in higher education : caring for self and
    others through challenging times / edited by Narelle Lemon, Heidi
    Harju-Luukkainen, and Susanne Garvis.
Other titles: Practicing compassion in higher education
Description: Abingdon, Oxon ; New York, NY : Routledge, 2023. |
    Series: Wellbeing and self-care in higher education | Includes
    bibliographical references and index.
Identifiers: LCCN 2022040138 (print) | LCCN 2022040139 (ebook) |
    ISBN 9781032326009 (hardback) | ISBN 9781032325996 (paperback) |
    ISBN 9781003315797 (ebook)
Subjects: LCSH: Universities and colleges—Health promotion services. |
    Compassion. | Self-care, Health. | Positive psychology. | College
    students—Mental health. | College teachers—Mental health. | Social
    distancing (Public health)—Pyschological aspects. | Social distancing
    (Public health) and education.
Classification: LCC LB2331.67.H4 P73 2023 (print) | LCC LB2331.67.H4
    (ebook) | DDC 378.1/97—dc23/eng/20221014
LC record available at https://lccn.loc.gov/2022040138
LC ebook record available at https://lccn.loc.gov/2022040139

ISBN: 978-1-032-32600-9 (hbk)
ISBN: 978-1-032-32599-6 (pbk)
ISBN: 978-1-003-31579-7 (ebk)

DOI: 10.4324/9781003315797

Typeset in Bembo
by Apex CoVantage, LLC

To our beautiful loved ones who have passed on, you are forever in our thoughts.

Contents

List of images	ix
List of tables	xii
List of contributors	xiii
Series preface	xviii
Acknowledgements	xxi

1 Caring for self and others through challenging times: interrupting the pandemic with compassion and kindness in higher education   1

NARELLE LEMON, HEIDI HARJU-LUUKKAINEN, AND SUSANNE GARVIS

SECTION 1
Kindness to self during COVID-19   13

2 "It be's that way sometime": mindfully recalling our time during COVID-19   15

LINDA NOBLE WITH MALGORZATA POWIETRZYNSKA

3 Generating the place of self-compassion in higher education: an academic place of belonging as a catalyst of the COVID-19 pandemic   33

NARELLE LEMON AND JOANNA HIGGINS

SECTION 2
Building compassion in our teaching during a pandemic   51

4 Cultivating compassion in higher education: international autoethnographic approach to online teaching during COVID-19   53

HEIDI HARJU-LUUKKAINEN, JONNA KANGAS, DAVID SMITH, MHAIRI
C BEATON, YLVA JANNOK NUTTI, AND RAUNI ÄÄRELÄ-VIHRIÄLÄ

viii *Contents*

5 **"It's gonna be alright": self-compassion for us and students during COVID-19** 67

GWEN ERLAM AND KAY HAMMOND

6 **Cultivating a language of compassion in higher education** 86

MAARIKA PIISPANEN AND MERJA MERILÄINEN

SECTION 3
The personal and professional blur: work-life family balance with COVID-19 101

7 **The personal and professional blur: work-life family balance with COVID-19** 103

TINA YNGVESSON, ANN-CHARLOTT WANK,
AND SUSANNE GARVIS

8 **Spaces to care and places to share: fostering a sense of belonging during the global pandemic through digitally mediated activity** 120

DONNA PENDERGAST, ALISON SAMMEL, LEONIE ROWAN, MIA
O'BRIEN, TRACEY MCCANN, HARRY KANASA, DAVID GEELAN,
BERYL EXLEY, CATHERINE DENNETT, AND SAKINAH ALHADAD

9 **Ethical responsibility in the struggle between the public and the private space: challenges and possibilities in teacher education during the pandemic** 148

MARITA CRONQVIST

Images

2.1	"Journeying towards wholeness" illustration by Dean Noble.	19
2.2	Savouring life's gifts.	23
2.3	Sketching a diorama with Cristina.	28
2.4	Enjoying mudras with Ken.	29
3.1	Melbourne pandemic timeline [Photos from top 29 January 2000, Singapore; 27 August 2020, Parliament Station escalators, Melbourne; 29 July 2021, vaccination two; and 9 January 2022, Brunswick supermarket carpark Melbourne].	36
3.2	New York adventures.	37
3.3 and 3.4	The beginning of our collaboration at roundtable conversations (2018 AERA).	39
3.5	Connecting and reminiscing about AERA at the airport with colleagues.	41
3.6	The dynamics of our collaboration.	43
3.7	Working virtually.	44
3.8	Screen conversations within text.	44
4.1	Visualising the empathy. Time to time I met students with my dog. Then the students dared to open their cameras with their cats and dogs around them as well.	57
4.2	This composite picture represents what COVID-19 meant to many academics from live presentations to working from our desk connecting via the internet.	58
4.3	This picture represents the ethos which our management sought to create during the pandemic that we were all "in it together" so that rather than viewing staff and students as separate entities, staff and students needed to support each other through the pandemic.	60
4.4	This picture visualises the exchange and collaboration connected to Sámi culture we tried to recreate online in our Sámi context. In the pictures you can see students gathered outside two lávvu used by the Sámi people. Picture Mattias Sikku Valio.	62
5.1	Visual narrative illustrating focus, strategy, and self-care routines.	68

x *Images*

5.2 Linking hope, goals, compassion, and wellbeing (Erlam). 70
5.3 Personal growth – use humour (Erlam). 74
5.4 Environmental mastery – train your mind (Erlam). 76
5.5 Autonomy – sail your ship (Hammond). 78
5.6 Autonomy, get moving – walk the dog (Erlam). 79
5.7 Purpose in life – give goals and light the way (Erlam). 81
5.8 Purpose in life – give goals and light the way (Erlam). 82
5.9 Model compassion – offer meaning and hope (Erlam). (Photo: Bruce Crossan, used with permission). 83
6.1 Shows the realisation of the study in the form of a short visual narrative. 87
6.2 The compassionate and supportive learning process during COVID-19. 96
7.1 Daily walks around the block. 106
7.2 Eating healthy and exercise. 107
7.3 Exercising together. 108
7.4 Feeling good after a lunch-time workout. 110
7.5 Making table decorations in the early afternoon. 111
7.6 Walking to "the office" with Vincent the Shih T'zu. 112
7.7 Defending my dissertation. 114
7.8 A lunch walk in the winter landscape. 115
7.9 Time for relaxing. 116
8.1 Going, going, gone. Campuses emptied and offices abandoned during the first phase of lockdown in Queensland, commencing 16 March 2020. 121
8.2 The strange becomes familiar: unfamiliar accessories, practices, and signage multiply. 122
8.3 School of Education and Professional Studies (EPS) Wellbeing Committee image, used for the EPS Work Family Facebook Group. 126
8.4 Flattening the curve – no probllama. 127
8.5 It's okay to turn your camera on: creating safe collegial spaces. 128
8.6 Where in the world is Stuart T. Llama, and what are those flowers he's smelling? 129
8.7 HMMDI's debut performance: AKA everything is better with a boa. 130
8.8 Moving our performances online – a shift from the physical to virtual space. 131
8.9 Sunshine comes from many places: bringing others into a musical fold. 133
8.10 Friday nights were not trivial. 134
8.11 Walking together through thick and thin, even when we're walking alone. 136
8.12 The idea to walk around Australia has been generated. 137
8.13 #DARCYDOG adventure. 138

Images xi

8.14	Voting on the route to be walked.	139
8.15	Imagining together.	140
8.16	Walking the room.	141
8.17	One of our walkers could walk no longer.	141
8.18	The finale – shared congratulations and shared celebrations.	142
8.19	Life goes on.	143
8.20	The authors, connected (in) still.	145
9.1	A visual representation of self-awareness through reflection.	150

Tables

6.1 Describes the Number of Students Enrolled in Each Course as well as the Averages of the Course Grades.   89

8.1 The Concept of Belonging – Five Themes Emerging from the Literature.   125

Contributors

Rauni Äärelä-Vihriälä is Associate Professor at Sámi Allaskuvla, Sámi University of Applied Sciences, Norway. She completed her doctoral dissertation in a unique study of Sámi language nest activities in 2016 from the University of Lapland. Professor Äärelä-Vihriälä's work at Sámi Allaskuvla focuses on the Sámi teacher education and the Sámi educational field of research. Her research focuses on Sámi language immersion.

Sakinah Alhadad is Senior Lecturer within the School of Education and Professional Studies at Griffith University. She joined the school because of a shared love of llamas and a genuine interest in the links between education and wellbeing.

Mhairi C Beaton is Professor in the Carnegie School of Education at Leeds Beckett University located in the United Kingdom. Mhairi's research focuses on the interface between inclusion, teacher education, and student voice.

Marita Cronqvist is Associate Professor of pedagogical work at the University of Borås. Her research areas are primarily future teachers' professional ethics and how students learn to take ethical responsibility in education. A didactic tool, Didethics, which draws attention to the ethical dimensions of teaching, has been developed based on research. The development of ethical leadership is investigated by combining didactics and digital tools in students' videopapers (reflections on recorded teaching). The research is largely conducted in the field of teacher training. Other areas covered in different studies are the importance of the body and emotions in teaching and learning. Methodologically, the research is primarily phenomenological with a basis in life world theory.

Catherine Dennett is Executive Support Officer for Initial Teacher Education Accreditation at Griffith University, and in her 18 years of working in the School of Education and Professional Studies has collected a significant number of plastic model dinosaurs.

Gwen Erlam is Senior Lecturer in the School of Public Health and Interprofessional Studies at Auckland University of Technology, New Zealand.

xiv *Contributors*

She is also a registered nurse working with cardiac patients from whom she draws much of her inspiration. She has studied distance and online education and has written six courses in online or blended formats for the University setting. These courses employ podcasts embedded with video clips to enhance engagement with students. She is an experienced educator teaching both undergraduate and post-graduate healthcare professionals by maximising pedagogical practices in simulated learning environments. These experiences give her a rich tapestry from which to draw on to encourage engagement and show empathy with students from different ages and in different learning spaces.

Beryl Exley is Deputy Head of the School of Education and Professional Studies at Griffith University and is Professor of English Curriculum and Literacies Education. She kept the EPS Work Fam Walk Around Australia tally during COVID-19.

Susanne Garvis (Griffith University) is a specialist in early childhood education and has been involved with many national and international projects around policy, quality, and learning with young children. Her most recent was a large meta-analysis exploring teacher qualifications and environmental quality. She has worked in many countries and currently lives in Australia.

David Geelan is National Head of the School of Education at the University of Notre Dame Australia and was Deputy Head of School (Academic) in the School of Education and Professional Studies at Griffith University during the pandemic. He has endearing passions for motorcycles, heavy metal music, and all things trivia.

Kay Hammond is Senior Lecturer in the School of Public Health and Interprofessional Studies, at Auckland University of Technology, New Zealand. She combines her backgrounds in education, psychology, language teaching, and performing art in her teaching and research. She obtained tertiary qualifications in psychology, TESOL, and higher education. She is an experienced learner within traditional, blended and online learning in Australia, Japan, and New Zealand. These experiences give her multidimensional empathy with students of different ages, language abilities, online/offline spaces, and wellbeing practices during higher education.

Heidi Harju-Luukkainen is Professor of education and Vice Director of Kokkola University Consortium Chydenius at the University of Jyväskylä, Finland. She also works as Professor of Education at Nord University, Norway and leads two international research groups and a doctoral program. She holds a PhD in education, special education teacher qualification, and a qualification in leadership and management from Finland. She has published more than 200 international books, journal articles, and reports as well as worked in multiple projects globally. Harju-Luukkainen has worked at top ranked universities in the USA like UCLA, USC as well as in many

Nordic research universities. She has developed education programs for universities, been a PI of PISA sub-assessments in Finland and functioned as a board professional. At the moment she is also a subject editor for the journal *Nordic Early Childhood Educational Research* and editorial board member for Educational Assessment and has published multiple books for international publishing houses during her career.

Joanna Higgins is Associate Professor and Associate Dean of Research in the Faculty of Education, Victoria University of Wellington, New Zealand. Joanna has taught in primary schools prior to joining the university as a teacher educator. Her research areas include: studies of classroom learning environments, professional inquiry and development, and wellbeing policy analysis and interventions including studies of mindfulness-based breathing in classrooms.

Harry Kanasa is Lecturer in the School of Education and Professional Studies. He is a gym junkie, avid foodie, and the creative musical director for #harrymademedoit, and occasionally fits in researching about STEAM inquiry.

Jonna Kangas has a PhD of education and is Adjunct Professor and University Lecturer and Joint Research Member in Playful Learning Center, Faculty of Education Science, University of Helsinki. Her research focus is on play-based pedagogy. She seeks to understand children's learning processes through joy and participation, and she uses her findings for designing innovative teacher training and mentoring programmes in Finland and developing countries. She is a director of blended teacher training program at the University of Helsinki.

Narelle Lemon is Professor and Associate Dean Education at Swinburne University of Technology in Melbourne, Australia. She is an internationally recognised researcher in education and initial teacher education bringing an interdisciplinarity across education, arts, and positive psychology. She engages with narrative inquiry and creative research methods with a recent focus on poetry, photography, and visual narratives. Her particular research expertise and interest relate to fostering wellbeing literacy in K–12 teachers, preservice teachers, and higher degree research students and academics in the higher education sector – that is, capacity building in wellbeing and self-care practices that supports proactive decision making across diverse evidence-based areas of wellbeing science in order to flourish while learning how to adapt to work, life, and societal stressors. Narelle tweets and grams as @rellypops, blogs as Wellbeing Whisperer, and can be found on Apple and Spotify with her various podcasts.

Tracey McCann is Technical Services Officer for the School of Education and Professional Studies at Griffith University, and a new grandma. She took up painting during the COVID-19 lockdowns. She is the voice of reason.

xvi *Contributors*

Merja Meriläinen, Positive Psychology Practitioner®, is Senior Lecturer, working as a primary school teacher trainer in adult teacher training in Kokkola University Consortium Chydenius. Student wellbeing, timely support for learning, compassionate guidance, and multi-located learning in authentic learning environments are interesting research topics from which she draws new tools for her teaching. She is an expert in positive psychology and a solution-focused coach, as well as a therapist specialising in emotional and art therapy work. Merja makes extensive use of this knowledge both in her research and in her work as a teacher educator.

Linda Noble and **Malgorzata Powietrzynska** are Adjunct Assistant Professors in the School of Education at Brooklyn College, City University of New York. They are corecipients of the 2018 Award for Excellence in Teaching for Part-Time Faculty at Brooklyn College. In addition their respective full time assignments are: a high school social studies teacher and a manager in a postsecondary educational institution. Linda and Malgorzata co-engage in research focusing on infusing contemplative practices into higher and secondary level education. Together they have spearheaded the creation of a Mindfulness Center in Linda's high school that is the site for mindfulness programming research, design, and implementation. Furthermore, they collaborate on providing professional development workshops in self-care and mindfulness to public school teachers in NYC. Their authored and co-authored publications include chapters in Malgorzata's co-edited volumes focused on mindfulness in everyday living. In recognition of her enriched classroom environment where social engagement is rooted in mindfulness, empathy, and appreciation of multiple perspectives Linda has received the Butler Cooley Excellence in Teaching Award and Long Island University Teacher of the Year Award.

Ylva Jannok Nutti is Associate Professor of Education and responsible for the Sámi Teacher Educations Master programs and Early Childhood Teacher Education Bachelor program and Prorector at Sámi allaskuvla/Sámi university of Applied Sciences.

Mia O'Brien is Senior Lecturer and Initial Teacher Education Director in the School of Education and Professional Studies at Griffith University, and spends her weekends pretending to be an artist, musician, and bookbinder.

Donna Pendergast is Dean and Head of the School of Education and Professional Studies at Griffith University and makes exceptional cumquat jam each July. She and her dogs did not miss one day of walking 10,000 steps during the lockdown – and she holds this record today.

Maarika Piispanen is a special class teacher and works as a university teacher in Kokkola University Consortium Chydenius in adult teacher training. The main areas of her work in preservice teacher training studies are linked with the following: pedagogical aspect in pre-primary and primary education, the development of learning in the authentic contextual-pedagogical environments, and individual learning and wellbeing in the aspect of art-based methods in elementary school environments. In recent years, Maarika's main research areas have concentrated on designing the learning environments with pedagogical and digital aspects, curriculum reform, individual learning and wellbeing and the early foreign language learning process.

Leonie Rowan is Professor and Director of the Griffith Institute for Educational Research at Griffith University and as the lead can't-sing-singer (cough . . . diva) of #harrymademedoit sports an endlessly glamorous wardrobe reflecting the belief that you can never have too many sequins.

Alison Sammel is Senior Lecturer in the School of Education and Professional Studies at Griffith University. She spent COVID-19 caring for (and adding to) her menagerie of fantastical beasts.

David Smith is the Head of Education at Charles Sturt University in Australia. He has developed a broad expertise in education through his work in schools and universities. David's research specialises in the fields of online learning and educational leadership working with education authorities globally.

Ann-Charlott Wank holds a PhD degree in education and works as a senior lecturer in early childhood education at the University of Borås. With her background as a preschool teacher, her research interest is in young children's learning and meaning-making, with a special focus on how communication influences children's opportunities to participate in meaning-making processes.

Tina Yngvesson is a lecturer in early childhood education at the University of Borås as well as a PhD research fellow in education at Nord University in Norway. Alongside various international and national research projects in early learning, child development and parental involvement in education, she also has a strong interest in the emergence of curriculum and the bridge between policy and praxis.

Series preface

As academics, scholars, staff, and colleagues working in the context of universities in the contemporary climate we are often challenged with where we place our own wellbeing. It is not uncommon to hear about burnout, stress, anxiety, pressures with workload, having too many balls in the air, toxic cultures, increasing demands, isolation, and feeling distressed (Berg and Seeber, 2016; Lemon & McDonough, 2018; Mountz et al., 2015). The reality is that universities are stressful places (Beer, et al., 2015; Cranton & Taylor, 2012; Kasworm & Bowles, 2012; Mountz et al., 2015; Ryan, 2013; Sullivan & Weissner, 2010; Wang & Cranton, 2012). McNaughton and Billot (2016) argue that the "deeply personal effects of changing roles, expectations and demands" (p. 646) have been downplayed and that academics and staff engage in constant reconstruction of their identities and work practices. It is important to acknowledge this, as much as it is to acknowledge the need to place wellbeing and self-care at the forefront of these lived experiences and situations.

Wellbeing can be approached at multiple levels including micro and macro. In placing wellbeing at the heart of the higher education workplace, self-care becomes an imperative both individually and systemically (Berg & Seeber, 2016; Lemon & McDonough, 2018). Self-care is most commonly oriented towards individual action to monitor and ensure personal wellbeing, however it is also a collective act. There is a plethora of different terms that are in action to describe how one approaches their wellbeing holistically (Godfrey et al., 2011). With different terminology comes different ways self-care is understood. For this collection self-care is understood as "the actions that individuals take for themselves, on behalf of and with others in order to develop, protect, maintain and improve their health, wellbeing or wellness" (Self Care Forum, 2019, para 1). It covers a spectrum of health-related (emotional, physical, and/or spiritual) actions including prevention, promotion, and treatment, while aiming to encourage individuals to take personal responsibility for their health and to advocate for themselves and others in accessing resources and care (Knapik & Laverty, 2018). Self-love, -compassion, -awareness, and -regulation are significant elements of self-care. But what does this look like for those working in higher education? In this book series authors respond to the questions: What do you do for self-care? How do you position wellbeing as part of your role in academia?

In thinking about these questions, authors are invited to critically discuss and respond to inspiration sparked by one or more of the questions of:

- How do we bring self-regulation to how we approach our work?
- How do we create a compassionate workplace in academia?
- What does it mean for our work when we are aware and enact self-compassion?
- What awareness has occurred that has disrupted the way we approach work?
- Where do mindful intentions sit?
- How do we shift the rhetoric of "this is how it has always been" in relation to overworking, and indiscretions between workload and approaches to workload?
- How do we counteract the traditional narrative of overwork?
- How do we create and sustain a healthier approach?
- How can we empower the "I" and "we" as we navigate self-care as a part of who we are as academics?
- How can we promote a curiosity about how we approach self-care?
- What changes do we need to make?
- How can we approach self-care with energy and promote shifts in how we work individually, collectively, and systemically?

The purpose of this book series is to:

- Place academic wellbeing and self-care at the heart of discussions around working in higher education.
- Provide a diverse range of strategies for how to put in place wellbeing and self-care approaches as an academic.
- Provide a narrative connection point for readers from a variety of backgrounds in academia.
- Highlight lived experiences and honour the voice of those working in higher education.
- Provide a visual narrative that supports connection to authors' lived experience(s).
- Contribute to the conversation on ways that wellbeing and self-care can be positioned in the work that those working in higher education do.
- Highlight new ways of working in higher education that disrupt current tensions that neglect wellbeing.

References

Beer, L. E., Rodriguez, K., Taylor, C., Martinez-Jones, N., Griffin, J., Smith, T. R., Lamar, M., & Anaya, R. (2015). Awareness, integration and interconnectedness. *Journal of Transformative Education*, *13*(2), 161–185.

Berg, M., & Seeber, B. K. (2016). *The slow professor: Challenging the culture of speed in the academy*. University of Toronto Press.

xx *Series preface*

Cranton, P., & Taylor, E. W. (2012). Transformative learning theory: Seeking a more unified theory. In E. W. Taylor & P. Cranton (Eds.), *The handbook of transformative learning* (pp. 3–20). Jossey-Bass.

Godfrey, C. M., Harrison, M. B., Lysaght, R., Lamb, M., Graham, I. D., & Oakley, P. (2011). The experience of self-care: A systematic review. *JBI Library of Systematic Reviews*, *8*(34), 1351–1460. www.ncbi.nlm.nih.gov/pubmed/27819888

Kasworm, C., & Bowles, T. (2012). Fostering transformative learning in higher education settings. In E. Taylor & P. Cranton (Eds.), *The handbook of transformative learning* (pp. 388–407). Sage.

Knapik, K., & Laverty, A. (2018). Self-care Individual, relational, and political sensibilities. In M. A. Henning, C. U. Krägeloh, R. Dryer, F. Moir, D. R. Billington, & A. G. Hill. (Eds.), *Wellbeing in higher education: Cultivating a healthy lifestyle among faculty and students.* Routledge.

Lemon, N., & McDonough, S. (Eds.). (2018). *Mindfulness in the academy: Practices and perspectives from scholars.* Springer.

McNaughton, S. M., & Billot, J. (2016). Negotiating academic teacher identity shifts during higher education contextual change. *Teaching in Higher Education, 21*(6), 644–658.

Mountz, A., Bonds, A., Mansfield, B., Loyd, J., Hyndman, J., & Watton-Roberts, M. (2015). For slow scholarship: A feminist politics of resistance through collective action in the neoliberal university. *ACME: An International E-Journal of Critical Geographies, 14*(4), 1235–1259.

Ryan, M. (2013). The pedagogical balancing act: Teaching reflection in higher education. *Teaching in Higher Education, 18*, 144–155.

Self Care Forum. (2019). *Self care forum: Home.* Retrieved July 27, 2019, from www.self careforum.org/

Sullivan, L. G., & Weissner, C. A. (2010). Learning to be reflective leaders: A case study from the NCCHC Hispanic leadership fellows program. In D. L. Wallin (Ed.), *Special issue: Leadership in an era of change. New directions for community colleges* (No. 149, pp. 41–50). Jossey-Bass.

Wang, V. C., & Cranton, P. (2012). Promoting and implementing Self-Directed Learning (SDL): An effective adult education model. *International Journal of Adult Vocational Education and Technology, 3*, 16–25.

Acknowledgements

To those who have kept us safe and provided us comfort as we navigate a pandemic. Be gentle.

1 Caring for self and others through challenging times

Interrupting the pandemic with compassion and kindness in higher education

Narelle Lemon, Heidi Harju-Luukkainen, and Susanne Garvis

Introduction

Essential to self-care is empowerment. This is required in both the daily practices we initiate and engage in, and additionally for the decisions we make that develop, maintain, and protect our wellbeing (Lemon, 2021). With self-care comes self-kindness, self-awareness, self-regulation, and self-compassion. At a time when there is incredible uncertainty exacerbated by the COVID-19 pandemic, the importance of valuing self-care has not changed (Lemon, 2021a, 2021b). What has come to light during the COVID-19 pandemic is that there are ways to take care of oneself and others where one can flourish or be true to their authentic self.

In this volume we think about self-care informed by positive psychology – to look at what is good in life where I, we, and us can flourish. To flourish is to find fulfilment in our lives, accomplishing meaningful and worthwhile tasks, and connecting with others at a deeper level – in essence, living the "good life" (Seligman, 2011). Flourishing is a state where people experience positive emotions, positive psychological functioning, and positive social functioning, most of the time, living within an optimal range of human functioning (Lomas et al., 2014), but the ways in which we engage with that value may need to have changed. But what does this mean for those who work in higher education especially at a time when the pandemic has highlighted the need for even more cuts to the sector, limitations of resources, shifts in how we work with each other and our students, and indeed the place of technology to facilitate connection? Critical currently is the place of self-care and especially the act of self-compassion.

Self-compassion involves being kind and understanding toward oneself rather than being harshly self-critical, even in instances of uncertainty, unknown, pain, failure, or worry (Neff, 2003). Self-compassion is a journey. On this journey the unexpected can emerge for us, and this can be activating. We close our hearts at this moment. That is a coping mechanism. During COVID-19 for many of us we have been confronted with the need to comfort ourselves, to soothe our self. There has been a need to be present,

DOI: 10.4324/9781003315797-1

enact a mindful awareness to allow for self-compassion to spring from the heart (Neff & Germer, 2018). Kristen Neff's work in self-compassion places mindful awareness, kindness to self, and common humanity as three central pillars. These are crucial for self-care. As such there is a need to engage with an awareness of what one needs and embraces when they have the chance to treat oneself more gently, or as they would a friend (Lemon, 2021). Mindfulness is vital in self-compassion to anchor awareness in the present moment (Neff & McGehee, 2010). Self-kindness has us being encouraging, supportive, unconditionally accepting. This is our soothing action to ourselves. And we can remind ourselves that everybody is complex, everybody is suffering and learning from their lived experiences. The common humanity pillar is a reminder that we all suffer, pain is a part of the shared human experience, and that every moment of suffering can be transformed into a moment of connection, with self and with others.

Those working in higher education are forever looking for ways to navigate the current climate and value self-care and wellbeing. COVID-19 has illuminated change and a system that both had existing issues regarding the place of wellbeing and self-care for those working in it, and that change will continue to occur underpinned by unknown, quick pivots, and reconsiderations to structures, access to resources and funding. As Marcia Devlin (2021) highlighted in her commentary "compassion and kindness aren't topics I've often heard discussed in universities in my 30 years in the sector" (para 6), and as such "I wonder if we might all find a bigger space for our humanity, our compassion and our kindness to each other" (para 8). As the higher education sector considers what a "COVID normal" university might look like, now is the time to consider the place of compassion and indeed self-compassion and when this will occur. Indeed, the pandemic has become a tipping point to reconsider who and what we want to be.

We draw on the work of Lemon and McDonough (2021) who wrote in response to COVID-19 and placing self-care and wellbeing at the heart of what we do – if not now, when? This volume explores, interrogates, and supports us to consider COVID-19, change and self-compassion in the higher education sector in relationship to self-care and wellbeing. Crucial to this is the place of self-compassion and the notations of awareness, kindness to self, and common humanity. We ask the questions: What does this mean in academia? How do we enact self-compassion at a time of change? How has the COVID-19 pandemic facilitated self-compassion, and what has the impact been on self and others? As such this book within the book series aims to:

- Discuss the impact of COVID-19 on academia and academics.
- Place academic wellbeing and self-care at the heart of discussions around working in higher education.
- Locate the place of self-compassion especially at a time of change and COVID-19.

- Provide a diverse range of voices, narratives, contexts, and strategies for how as an academic to put in place wellbeing and self-care approaches underpinned by self-compassion.
  Provide a narrative connection point for readers from a variety of backgrounds in academia.
- Provide a visual narrative that supports connection to authors' lived experience(s).
- Contribute to the conversation on ways that wellbeing and self-care can be positioned in the work that academics do.
- Highlight new ways of working in higher education that disrupt current tensions that neglect wellbeing.

To assist in this inquiry with curiosity and courage we have framed questions across intersecting sections. This forms the how the book is divided, with each of the three sections and their underpinning questions providing starting points for each author(s) as well as you as a reader:

Kindness to self during COVID-19

What does it mean to be an academic during COVID-19?
How do we enact self-compassion at a time of change due to the COVID-19 pandemic?
What has kindness looked like?
What kinds of kindness have carried forward beyond lockdowns?

Building compassion in our teaching during a pandemic

How has the COVID-19 pandemic facilitated self-compassion, and what has the impact been on self and others in relation to teaching?
How have we shown humanity and kindness to ourselves and our students?

The personal and professional blur: work–life family balance with COVID-19

How has the COVID-19 pandemic facilitated self-compassion, and what has the impact been on self and others in relation to family structures?
What has kindness and humanity looked like at this time?

Kindness to self during COVID-19

The pandemic has allowed us to pause. To reflect. To be uncomfortable. It has been as confronting as it has been an opportunity to explore what can be possible when we do things differently. What we have noticed during the pandemic is the need to care. To care for self and each other. And for many of us to care in different ways. In the context of higher education this has been paramount as we individually and collectively process the significant changes to what it means to be human. We have navigated changes in how we enact and embody our work. We have had to humanise the virtual classrooms and spaces we teach, research, and meet in while creating spaces where we care for each other across modalities (Christopher & Watson, 2020; Wampole & Kohli, 2022). We have had to (re)conceptualise what "being there" means (Ekmekci, 2013, p. 29) in terms of engagement, relationships, safety, accessibility, inclusivity, and the cultivation of strengths-based practices and opportunities to flourish. The creation of cultures to allow us to understand and improve systems, to interrupt toxic leadership that promotes overwork, and to prioritise physical and mental wellbeing that is underpinned by empathy (Binagwaho, 2020; Hofmeyer et al., 2020) whereby "self-care will be an easier choice for staff" (Hofmeyer et al., 2020, p. 3) *has had to be essential*. Kindness and compassion have had to be a part of cultural shifts as we care deeply for each other (Cordaro, 2020), and as we have constructed a shared empathy and stronger kindness for one another (Allen et al., 2020). In doing so we have had to think about the impact of compassion in partnership with change and COVID-19. As we have shifted towards valuing compassion, we have voted for our subjective wellbeing, with significant positive impact on autonomy, competence, and relatedness (Gherghel et al, 2021). This we can argue is something higher education and the academy can always benefit from.

Compassion comes with self-compassion, kindness, empathy, gratitude, and appreciation as prosocial acts that impact not only those on the receiving end, but also those embodying. In the workplace, there is a flow on effect for efficiency, success, positive relationships, and individual wellbeing (Datu et al., 2022; Di Fabio et al., 2017). As we care for ourselves, we care for others. This is something the pandemic has most certainly called on us to (re)consider. We have been called upon to promote different ways of working and being. With this comes a self-compassion, a need to be kind to ourselves as we process what is happening around us and to ourselves personally and professionally. As Neff (2010) reminds us, self-compassion as a emotionally positive self-attitude can protect us against the negative consequences of self-judgement, isolation, and rumination and entails three main components:

> (a) self-kindness – being kind and understanding toward oneself in instances of pain or failure rather than being harshly self-critical, (b) common humanity – perceiving one's experiences as part of the larger human experience rather than seeing them as separating and isolating, and (c) mindfulness – holding painful thoughts and feelings in balanced awareness rather than over-identifying with them.
>
> (p. 85)

It is the transitioning through, across, and within uncertain times that we have all had to renegotiate our lives and work. In this section of the book we hear from two collaborations that have been reflexive of the experiences of the pandemic as a way to move beyond siloed, and at times narrow facing and insular, ways of thinking and being. We are invited as readers to engage with chapters that have seen benefits coming out of challenges with a humanising of experiences that values (self-)awareness and collective belonging.

Linda Noble with Malgorzata Powietrzynska model for us a shared vulnerability that comes with a kindness to lean into relationships where you can be raw, open, and experience a common humanity. With New York and the pandemic as a backdrop to their experiences, we are guided through how we can approach and process the amplification of life and death. Their exploration of care and a sense of belonging is passed onto the following chapter by Narelle Lemon and Joanna Higgins, who explore the interruption that has come from international collaborations and the seeking of connection across the international borders of Melbourne, Australia and Wellington, New Zealand. By prioritising connecting and sustaining their time together, they have shifted the continual othering of each other that is so strong in the academy. As a paradigm shift of what is valued in the academy, we are invited to engage with a chapter that places belonging, care, self-care, and self-compassion at the forefront of collaboration, interrupting the traditional "markers of success of local, national and international that are so commonly positioned as important for progression of career trajectory . . . where international publishing, attending conferences, and collaborating can only be carried out face-to-face" (Lemon and Higgins, in this collection). Both chapters highlight for us the valuing of relationship to wellbeing in the academy where connection is possible, as to is avoidance of "getting stuck in "me" versus "them" or alternate self-absorbed forms of othering" (Noble and Powietrzynska, this collection).

Building compassion in our teaching during a pandemic

The COVID-19 pandemic has changed the way we look at teaching and learning. The pandemic forced higher education to learn new technologies, to transform into remote teaching, and to adapt quickly to new realities by adapting pedagogical practices. These changes had to happen on multiple levels in higher education, ranging from the administration to the pedagogical practices. These quick changes were a clear stress factor for many teachers and some were expressing a desire to go back to the "normal" as soon as possible. However, Bartholomay (2021) argues that teaching during COVID-19 has presented opportunities for educators to become more compassionate towards their students. Further, Hess et al. (2021) highlight that these challenges experienced during COVID-19, underline the importance of care-informed pedagogy in education. The compassion can be present in the ways teachers restructure their courses or for instance make education accessible for vulnerable groups. According to Gillis and Krull (2020) which instructional technique instructors use is less important than how well they implement it for students' learning. Further, the authors argue that teaching during a global pandemic makes even clearer the importance of communication and accessibility as well as the need

6 *Narelle Lemon, Heidi Harju-Luukkainen and Susanne Garvis*

to be aware of barriers (both anticipated and unanticipated) that may arise to negatively impact students' learning. A recent study conducted by Egan et al. (2022) indicated a strong clear association between better academic performance and higher resiliency, mindfulness, self-compassion, and consideration of future consequences, and further a negative association to procrastination. Therefore, building a compassionate higher education environment is not, and should not only be a task of individual teachers but rather a goal for the entire academic community.

Therefore, rather than abandoning the lessons learned during the pandemic, we should focus on how we can find opportunities to incorporate what we have learned about the importance of compassion into teaching in higher education. This section will take a closer look at how teachers were building compassion with their students during the pandemic, from multiple viewpoints and also across the globe. The section will answer questions like how has the COVID-19 pandemic facilitated self-compassion, and what has the impact been on self and others in relation to teaching? How have we shown humanity and kindness to ourselves and towards our students? It is clear, while looking at these notions, that the higher education post-COVID-19 futures are many. It becomes therefore even clearer that now we need to reimagine our future in higher education and to flexibly develop our working practices towards the future we want to imagine – towards a future that is a more compassionate one (see also Eringfeld, 2020).

The first chapter of this section (Chapter 4) is called *Cultivating compassion in higher education: international autoethnographic approach to online teaching during COVID-19* by Heidi Harju-Luukkainen, Jonna Kangas, David Smith, Ylva Jannok Nutti and Mhairi C Beaton. In this chapter the authors take a closer look at their experiences as academics, when they tried to cultivate compassion amongst their students during COVID-19, while teaching in higher education. The textual and visual data of this study come from four different countries and higher educational contexts. According to the results, students in higher education were supported in multiple ways, on three different levels in the academic context (administrational, operational, and individual). In their chapter they also highlight four practical outcomes for future work with students during a crisis. The fifth chapter, called *"It's gonna be alright": self-compassion for us and students during COVID-19*, is authored by Gwen Erlam and Kay Hammond. The context for this chapter is two academic course leaders in lockdown, while concurrently dealing with unavoidable pandemic challenges like anxiety and depression and how they found solace in online platforms. The authors describe how they communicated with students in ways intended to guide them towards healthier wellbeing. They also describe how they used images and personal stories to demonstrate compassion. The sixth chapter is called *Cultivating a language of compassion in higher education*, written by Merja Meriläinen and Maarika Piispanen. It explores the experiences of two teacher educators creating and planning compassionate study modules amidst the changed circumstances. The chapter illuminates how we can find

Caring for self and others through challenging times   7

positive factors in a changed situation and how positive factors can reinforce the resilience of students in higher education. They argue that wellbeing does not need to disappear in altered circumstances, but it does require compassion and compassionate language to survive.

The personal and professional blur: work-life family balance with COVID-19

In the next section of the book we read chapters exploring *work-life family balance with COVID-19*. Across the three chapters, strategies and reflections are given on the pivot to working from home and how there was a new creation of boundaries. This also included relationships with family (including children) and pets.

In Chapter 7 (Yngvesson, Wank & Garvis), the *Personal and Professional Blur* is shared across two different countries, Sweden and Australia. The authors acknowledge that the pandemic is a marathon and not a sprint, requiring many adaptations to teaching and learning over a longer duration of time (Unadkat & Farquhar, 2020). As such, the first theme across the visual imagery of the writers was around the importance of movement and health as a self-care strategy. The team reflected on the possibilities of poor health practices by sitting at home at a desk and acknowledged the importance of moving to help support resiliency and continued wellbeing across the pandemic. For some this meant exercising at home, while for others it included walks in the fresh air.

Another key reflection from the authors was the continued blurring of boundaries between roles, relationships, and processes that were continued to be re-established and negotiated as part of the marathon of the pandemic. Prior routines were no longer possible and continual change had to be accepted and acknowledged to support ongoing change. The continuous change also helped move beyond work becoming monotonous to more meaningful ways of working. This approach also allowed for "moments of happiness and other positive emotions occur every day even during a pandemic, but we often fail to absorb and internalize them" (Norcross & Phillips, 2020, p. 61).

Chapter 8 presents *Spaces to care and places to share: fostering a sense of belonging during the global pandemic through digitally mediated activity* (Pendergast, Sammel, Rowan, O'Brien, McCann, Kanasa, Geelan, Exley, Dennett, and Alhadad), where strategies are provided during lockdowns and transitions to working from home. Such shifts with loss of boundaries between home and work, home and school, leisure and work had been described as a distinctive cultural shift (Pendergast & Deagon, 2021). Over a period of time, visual artefacts were collected to show insights in often challenging ways (Exley & Cottrel, 2012). Initiated activities designed to address the uncertainties of the moment included weekly virtual staff meetings, musical performances, establishment of a work family Facebook group that gave people multiple ways to connect including a virtual Walk Around Australia club and a weekly trivia evening.

8 *Narelle Lemon, Heidi Harju-Luukkainen and Susanne Garvis*

At the end of the chapter, the writing team also realise that the pandemic is not over, and acknowledge a prolonged sense of liminality within an end in sight. However, there is strong acknowledgement of the importance of a place that values connectedness and a sense of belonging, where positive ways forward are acknowledged when self-care is centre.

In the final chapter, Cronqvist discusses ethical responsibility between the public and private space. The author shares strategies for responsible reflective learning environments including active dialogue with preservice teacher learning from the home environment. Another strategy includes self-awareness about values and attitudes between on campus and school with video paper (Cronqvist, 2019, 2021). As such, there is a great call for humanity, self-care, and wellbeing during a pivot to the digitalisation of learning. This also includes reflections on understanding synchronous and asynchronous learning when working with preservice teachers, where a balance between the public and private space is needed. This approach also relies on role models for preservice teachers and courage to engage in reflective learning.

Concluding remarks

What each of the chapters in this book illuminates is what is beginning to emerge in the research coming out of the pandemic. That is, for those who found meaning amongst the grief, shock, trauma, fear, upheaval, change, and uncertainty of the pandemic a certain level of control, self-esteem, and belonging have been able to be cultivated individually and amongst others. The ability to be altruistic, supportive, and practical with peers, friends, family, and/or community have provided means to calibrate and refrain any sense of negativity (Matos et al., 2021; Polizzi et al., 2020; Nader et al., 2020; Waters et al., 2022). The ability to be able to bounce back and be content with the everydayness of fluctuating circumstances has been able to lessen the burden of imposed distress, something we have learned from other mass traumas in our world (for example Askari et al., 2022; Bonanno et al., 2010; Fredrickson et al., 2003; Polizzi et al., 2020; Smith et al., 2011; Waters et al., 2022). The pandemic in this sense can be seen as a tipping point whereby we locate compassion and self-compassion as what we do.

The narratives and visual narratives shared are powerful reminders of the social and relational aspect of wellbeing and self-care. The self aspect of self-care indeed has us being aware, present and kind in order to care for others: our peers, colleagues, students, friends, loved ones, and community. We are invited to engage with lived experiences where connection to storytelling enables us to also embrace what might be possible. In this case we are invited to consider the place of compassion amongst change and the pandemic. We are invited to draw meaning from proactive strategies that have helped with compassion, change, and the pandemic. And we are asked to be courageous, to try and explore while being curious into the significance and richness of the visual narratives and narratives that are provided that reveal for us the complexity of academic identity.

Our colleagues, the authors in this book, enable us to extend and deepen our insights into our own journey with the place of self-care and wellbeing.

The process of coming to writing about lived experiences and wellbeing, and indeed the writing process itself, may be a part of a cathartic journey for authors. This book is more than this though. It is about sharing lived experiences that help others. We learn from stories. We connect, resolve, rethink, explore, inquire, take action and become inspired. The telling and retelling helps us find meaning, as too does the listening and relistening. It is hoped that this book, and the book series, helps some of you make connections in your own self-care routines, habits, and practices. Collectively we highlight the need to shift our assumptions and expectations that make people feel like their wellbeing is something to put to the side. And it is the sharing of narratives connected to explicit proactive strategies that becomes an interruption to traditional narratives of overwork, poor health, stress, exhaustion, burnout, and no self-care. Most importantly during a significant moment in history, COVID-19, compassion, and change are three "c" words that indeed have accompanied us into the new decade but offer so much for us in how we move forward.

References

Allen, J., Rowan, L., & Singh, P. (2020). Teaching and teacher education in the time of COVID-19, *48*(3), 233–236. https://doi.org/10.1080/1359866X.2020.1752051

Askari, I., Wenglorz, L., Gajewski, F. J., Jänner, M., Vetter, A., Askari, A., Askari, S., Balázsy, Z., Bramer-Ugur, S., Reinermann, D., Nolting, T., Meisenzahl, E., & Kujovic, M. (2022). Predicting the role of coping factors on pandemic-related anxiety. *Current Psychology (New Brunswick, N.J.)*, 1–10. https://doi.org/10.1007/s12144-022-03188-7

Bartholomay, D. J. (2022). A time to adapt, not "return to normal": Lessons in compassion and accessibility from teaching during COVID-19. *Teaching Sociology*, *50*(1), 62–72. https://doi.org/10.1177/0092055X211053376

Binagwaho, A. (2020). We need compassionate leadership management based on evidence to defeat COVID-19. *International Journal of Health Policy and Management*, *9*(10), 413–414. https://doi.org/10.34172/IJHPM.2020.73

Bonanno, G. A., Brewin, C. R., Kaniasty, K., & la Greca, A. M. (2010). Weighing the costs of disaster: Consequences, risks, and resilience in individuals, families, and communities. *Psychological Science in the Public Interest: A Journal of the American Psychological Society*, *11*(1), 1–49. https://doi.org/10.1177/1529100610387086

Christopher, R., de Tantillo, L., & Watson, J. (2020). Academic caring pedagogy, presence, and Communitas in nursing education during the COVID-19 pandemic. *Nursing Outlook*, *68*(6), 822–829. https://doi.org/10.1016/J.OUTLOOK.2020.08.006

Cordaro, M. (2020). View of pouring from an empty cup: The case for compassion fatigue in higher education. *Building Healthy Academic Communities*, *4*(2), 1–12. https://library.osu.edu/ojs/index.php/BHAC/article/view/7618/5794

Cronqvist, M. (2019). Reflecting and verbalizing teaching – supported by didactic and digital tools. *Beijing International Review of Education*, *1*(2–3), 512–532.

Cronqvist, M. (2021). Embodied becoming – student teachers' reflections on their filmed teaching. *Video Journal of Education and Pedagogy*, *6*(1), 1–16. https://doi.org/10.1163/23644583-bja10017

Datu, J. A. D., Buenconsejo, J. U., Valdez, J. P. M., & Tang, R. L. (2022). Gratitude and kindness at work as predictors of employees' mental health outcomes during the COVID-19 pandemic. *Psychology, Health & Medicine*. https://doi.org/10.1080/1354850 6.2022.2079690

Devlin, M. (2021). *Making space for compassion*. https://srheblog.com/2021/04/08/making-space-for-compassion/

di Fabio, A., Palazzeschi, L., & Bucci, O. (2017, November). Gratitude in organizations: A contribution for healthy organizational contexts. *Frontiers in Psychology, 8*, 2025. https://doi.org/10.3389/FPSYG.2017.02025/BIBTEX

Egan, H., O'Hara, M., Cook, A., & Mantzios, M. (2022). Mindfulness, self-compassion, resiliency and wellbeing in higher education: A recipe to increase academic performance. *Journal of Further and Higher Education, 46*(3), 301–311. doi:10.1080/0309877X. 2021.1912306

Ekmekci, O. (2013). Being there: Establishing instructor presence in an online learning environment. *Higher Education Studies, 3*(1). https://doi.org/10.5539/hes.v3n1p29

Eringfeld, S. (2021). Higher education and its post-coronial future: Utopian hopes and dystopian fears at Cambridge University during Covid-19. *Studies in Higher Education, 46*(1), 146–157. doi:10.1080/03075079.2020.1859681

Exley, B., & Dooley, K. (2015). Critical linguistics in the early years: Exploring language functions through sophisticated picture books and process drama strategies. In K. Winograd (Ed.), *Critical literacies and young learners: Connecting classroom practice to the common core* (pp. 128–143). Routledge.

Fredrickson, B. L., Tugade, M. M., Waugh, C. E., & Larkin, G. R. (2003). What good are positive emotions in crises? A prospective study of resilience and emotions following the terrorist attacks on the United States on September 11th, 2001. *Journal of Personality and Social Psychology, 84*(2), 365. https://doi.org/10.1037/0022-3514.84.2.365

Gherghel, C., Nastas, D., Hashimoto, T., & Takai, J. (2021). The relationship between frequency of performing acts of kindness and subjective well-being: A mediation model in three cultures. *Current Psychology, 40*(9), 4446–4459. https://doi.org/10.1007/S12144-019-00391-X/FIGURES/1

Gillis, A., & Krull, L. M. (2020). COVID-19 remote learning transition in spring 2020: Class structures, student perceptions, and inequality in college courses. *Teaching Sociology, 48*(4), 283–299. https://doi.org/10.1177/0092055X20954263

Hess, K., McAuliffe, E. L., Gleckman-Krut, M., & Shapiro, S. (2022). Learning from 2020: How the challenges of remote teaching reinforce the need for care-informed pedagogy. *Teaching Sociology, 50*(1), 3–16. https://doi.org/10.1177/0092055X211060344

Hofmeyer, A., Taylor, R., & Kennedy, K. (2020). Fostering compassion and reducing burnout: How can health system leaders respond in the Covid-19 pandemic and beyond? *Nurse Education Today, 94*, 104502. https://doi.org/10.1016/J.NEDT.2020.104502

Lemon, N. (2021a). Illuminating five possible dimensions of self-care during the COVID-19 pandemic. *International Health Trends and Perspectives, 1*(2), 161–175. https://doi.org/10.32920/IHTP.V1I2.1426

Lemon, N. (2021b). Self-care is worthy of our attention: Using our self-interest for good in higher education. In N. Lemon (Ed.), *Creating a Place for Self-care and Wellbeing in Higher Education* (pp. 1–9). Routledge. https://doi.org/10.4324/9781003144397-1

Lemon, N., & McDonough, S. (2021). If not now, then when? Wellbeing and wholeheartedness in education, *85*(3), 317–335. https://doi.org/10.1080/00131725.2021.1912231

Lomas, T., Heffferon, K., & Ivatzan, I. (2014). *Applied positive psychology: Integrated positive practice*. Sage Publications Inc.

Matos, M., McEwan, K., Kanovský, M., Halamová, J., Steindl, S. R., Ferreira, N., Linharel-hos, M., Rijo, D., Asano, K., Vilas, S. P., Márquez, M. G., Gregório, S., Brito-Pons, G., Lucena-Santos, P., da Silva Oliveira, M., de Souza, E. L., Llobenes, L., Gumiy, N., Costa, M. I., . . . Gilbert, P. (2021). The role of social connection on the experience of COVID-19 related post-traumatic growth and stress. *PLoS One, 16*(12), e0261384. https://doi.org/10.1371/JOURNAL.PONE.0261384

Mohammadpour, M., Ghorbani, V., Khoramnia, S., Ahmadi, S. M., Ghvami, M., & Maleki, M. (2020). Anxiety, self-compassion, gender differences and COVID-19: Predicting self-care behaviors and fear of COVID-19 based on anxiety and self-compassion with an emphasis on gender differences. *Iranian Journal of Psychiatry, 15*(3), 213. https://doi.org/10.18502/IJPS.V15I3.3813

Neff, K. (2003). Self-compassion: An alternative conceptualization of a healthy attitude toward oneself. *Self and Identity, 2*, 85–102. https://doi.org/10.1080/15298860390129863

Neff, K. (2010). Self-compassion: An alternative conceptualization of a healthy attitude toward oneself. *Self and Identity, 2*(2), 85–101. https://doi.org/10.1080/15298860309032

Neff, K., & Germer, C. (2018). *The mindful self-compassion workbook: A proven way to accept yourself, build inner strength, and thrive.* Guilford Press. www.guilford.com/books/The-Mindful-Self-Compassion-Workbook/Neff-Germer/9781462526789

Neff, K., & McGehee, P. (2010). Self-compassion and psychological resilience among adolescents and young adults. *Self and Identity, 9*(3), 225–240. https://doi.org/10.1080/15298860902979307

Norcross, J. C., & VandenBos, G. R. (2018). *Leaving it at the office*: A guide to psychotherapist self-care (2nd ed.). Guilford Press.

Pendergast, D., & Deagon, J. R. (2021). Home economics, the COVID-19 global pandemic and beyond. *International Journal of Home Economics, 14*(2), 2–15. www.ifhe.org/filead min/user_upload/e_Journal/vol_14_1/P1_Pendergast-Deagon.pdf

Polizzi, C., Lynn, S. J., & Perry, A. (2020). Stress and coping in the time of Covid-19: Pathways to resilience and recovery. *Clinical Neuropsychiatry, 17*(2), 59. https://doi.org/10.36131/CN20200204

Salari, N., Hosseinian-Far, A., Jalali, R., Vaisi-Raygani, A., Rasoulpoor, S., Mohammadi, M., Rasoulpoor, S., & Khaledi-Paveh, B. (2020). Prevalence of stress, anxiety, depression among the general population during the COVID-19 pandemic: A systematic review and meta-analysis. *Globalization and Health, 16*(1). https://doi.org/10.1186/S12992-020-00589-W

Seligman, M. E. P. (2011). *Flourish.* Random House Australia.

Smith, W., Davies-Colley, C., Mackay, A., & Bankoff, G. (2011). Social impact of the 2004 Manawatu floods and the "hollowing out" of rural New Zealand. *Disasters, 35*(3), 540–553. https://doi.org/10.1111/j.1467-7717.2011.01228.x

Unadkat, S., & Farquhar, M. (2020). Doctors' wellbeing: Self-care during the covid-19 pandemic. *BMJ, 368*, m1150. doi:10.1136/bmj.m1150

Wampole, D. M., & Kohli, H. (2022). Self-compassion in social work education at times of COVID19, *20*(4), 400–417. https://doi.org/10.1080/15332985.2022.2028218

Waters, L., Algoe, S. B., Dutton, J., Emmons, R., Fredrickson, B. L., Heaphy, E., Moskow-itz, J. T., Neff, K., Niemiec, R., Pury, C., & Steger, M. (2021). Positive psychology in a pandemic: Buffering, bolstering, and building mental health, *17*(3), 303–323. https://doi.org/10.1080/17439760.2021.1871945

Section 1

Kindness to self during COVID-19

2 "It be's that way sometime"

Mindfully recalling our time during COVID-19

Linda Noble with Malgorzata Powietrzynska

The soil from which we grow

This autoethnographic research (Wall, 2006) emerged during the initial implementation of a course curriculum designed by the co-authors of this paper. Our course focuses on the theory and practice of mindfulness (a special quality of attention; Kabat-Zinn, 1994), which research has shown to support personal, communal, and societal wellbeing (e.g., MLERN, 2012). By elevating the importance of socio-emotional and mental health, the course content aligns with what Ladson-Billings (2021) refers to as "the hard re-set" in the way we approach education post-pandemic.

We describe how we co-constructed a more equitable learning environment through relinquishing power while centring identity, agency, belonging, and collaboration, i.e., the focal constructs of transformative socio-emotional learning (Jagers et al., 2021). Guided by our students, we shifted from a "pedagogy of compliance" (Hammond, 2021) to co-create space for each other to authentically show up and compassionately bear witness to our humanity. Of salience were our respective multidimensional and intersectional positionalities; two white middle-aged female professors working with a cohort of undergraduate students of colour, from historically disadvantaged communities.

Our work is grounded in concepts of social justice which are prominent in holistic education (Luvmour, 2021). Furthermore, we value culturally responsive education that positions students to become leaders of their own learning (Hammond, 2021). Finally, we draw from research on the benefits of socio-emotional learning (see Jagers et al., 2021). From within this theoretical framework our approach was to engage in reflection after each course session to analyse difficult event(s) and emotions that resonated within and between us. We gathered information from sources that included students' journal reflections, reading responses, projects, conversations, academic advisory updates, and intangible behaviours of body language evident in action as well as inaction. Guided by the principles of authentic inquiry (Tobin, 2015), as we embraced vulnerability (Brown, 2012) to recognise the deficits in our pedagogical approach, we fearlessly began to adopt a more equitable pedagogy

DOI: 10.4324/9781003315797-3

to benefit the collective. As "teachers", we discerned and let go of our attachment to expectations (Koffman, 2012).

We embraced the lived experience of the individual in order to situate the wholeness of self and afford a sense of belonging as a foundation for equity and engagement in learning (Jagers et al., 2021). We aspired to build capacity for personal agency by decentring and by redistributing power. We are interested in content as a disruptive material as well as types of assessment that can challenge the traditional understanding of knowledge and intelligence, in essence what it means "to know". We are curious about developing skills that are essential to wellbeing. We are committed to valuing the human experience by exploring and co-engaging in authentic dialogue about the content of internal reflection (Ergas, 2017). Overall, our pedagogical approach became transformed by ontological shifts (Tobin, 2015) that embraced learning situated in relationships and values our interbeing (Nhất Hạnh, 2017) as a pathway forward.

A roadmap for the journey ahead

Perched on a ledge in the cavernous circle of existence, we wonder about the significant events of circumstance, specifically, when the indiscriminate interloper COVID-19 inaugurated inferno. The diabolical dis-ease usurped freedom as it wantonly cast a shadow, masking hope and aspiration on the face of humanity. Has this or other circumstance waged a coup to cloud your mind, or crush your spirit? Are you in mental, physical, or emotional pain? We see you. We feel you. We are connected in our humanity.

This chapter is a reflection upon the multiple identities we assume as we engage in enacting social life. To that end, we explore three major themes. First, we each tell a tale of our lived experience as mothers, daughters, wives, and members of communities discussing the evolution of our respective approaches to individual self-care. Next, as long-time coteachers and friends for whom compassion and caring for each other has been a source of strength, we dive into describing how we embodied and leaned into kindness with each other in our relationship. Finally, we share the manner in which the global pandemic reshaped our approach to self-care in building relationships with and learning alongside our students.

In each section the COVID-19 experience is viewed through the lens of the challenges it posed. At the same time, and perhaps more importantly, we highlight the opportunities that emerged as we were reframing our way of being in the world. We ground our narrative in the work of practitioners and advocates for self-care. Among others, we apply Tara Brach's concept of RAIN (Recognize, Allow, Investigate, Nurture) for radical compassion. Furthermore, we elevate the power of vulnerability as framed by Brené Brown. Finally, Kristin Neff's work provides a lens to investigate being compassionate to imperfection towards healing destructive emotional patterns for inner peace and happiness.

Linda's story of holding and healing

Against the backdrop of COVID-19, I share with you the strain, the pain, and the joy that grows from holding love in a healing life. I am blessed to be held in the arms of brother patience, while healing sister gratitude uplifts my spirit. Come. May you too feel compassion to rise above duality and lovingly embrace darkness, knowing that nothing is neither good nor bad, just is.

To provide immediate context, I will begin with my pre-COVID-19 back story that spans decades of teaching, earning multiple degrees, yet drastically devoid of Tara Brach's radical acceptance (2004) or radical compassion (2020). I had truly mastered dis-ease. I was a ticking time bomb taking three trips to the ER, stockpiling stress in my spine as Bessel Van Der Kolk (2015) helped me understand.

In response to stress I have indulged, specifically in habits of judgement, impatience, quitting on myself, and running on empty. As a wife and a mother, I dragged myself through the "daze" and never really experienced the moments in relationship with myself or my loved ones. I was distant from my true nature. I enveloped the helpless shame of being mindlessly absent. At times the path of least resistance seemed to be sinking into the toxic comfort of a familiar circumstance – self-harm, self-denial, or disconnect as referenced by Tabitha Mpamira-Kaguri's (2019) in her wisdom that trauma not transformed is trauma transferred.

Furthermore, I have been haunted by echoes of judgement – "not good enough" that emanate in part from an unsettled self-image as a rootless immigrant, burdened with what Dena Simmons (2016) refers to as an imposter syndrome. Born in London of Irish immigrants, I wanted to glisten in the flickering light emanating from the distant New York City skyline. Blindly, I clawed my way through the clouds of the monochromatic patriarchy and stifling dogma of century-old institutions to arrive in NYC. While bearing the privilege of a white European female, on occasion my hardship was exposed. For example, early in my career an administrator hiring for a faculty position failed to see beyond his primary aversion to my waiting tables to pay for the cost of tuition. He snarled that I had taken "too long" to graduate with a self-financed doctorate. I recoiled, recalling the long nights and innumerable meals I had served to strangers for small change. While gaslighting (Stark, 2019), he refused to acknowledge my glaring academic credentials and blatant resilience. At that time, I was afraid to show my true emotion. Now, in hindsight, I appreciate the circumstance, and with great humility and dignity connect with my graduate students on a bridge of resilience and financial hardship at the intersection of our lived experiences.

Mindfulness practice has helped me to ameliorate stress in my life. Being aware of the fleeting nature of emotion and recognising my own foolishness, I have come to experience the transformative nature of mindfulness for everyday living. First, let me catch your ear with Parker Palmer's (2004) words about doing the inner work – the work before the work. In healing, I have slowly

18 *Linda Noble with Malgorzata Powietrzynska*

begun the process of releasing control by erasing a lifetime of pictures. Below are a few examples that illustrate early enactments of my fragmented life.

Act I Picture a child bereft with survivor's guilt self-soothing with music (a symphony of anguish) to silence the whispers of six deceased siblings miscarried and stillborn.

Act II Picture a girl with an accent battling bulimia to disembody from the weight of oppression she carries shrouded by insecurity of being "the foreigner".

Act III Picture a female student in an all-male undergraduate business class drowning each time she attempts to navigate the rapids of the college cafeteria recalling Audrey Lorde's (1997) words, "We operate in the teeth of a system for whom racism and sexism are primary, established, and necessary props of profit" (p. 281).

Act IV Picture a night worker returning alone to her studio, a victim mugged twice for tips; an uninsured survivor from a NYC bicycle accident with both arms encasted.

Act V Picture a 40-year-old woman, single, barren, and loveless.

Act VI Picture a mid-40s unemployed graduate asking, Where am I going?

I recognise that we move through life with the shadow of struggle and carry the light of our ancestral spirit. Embracing both, I am grateful for Nora, a grandmother with a heart of gold who bore fourteen children, one of whom Helga gifted me with life for which I chose the road less travelled! Yet, despite the intellectual cognition of circumstance, a sinkhole or a boulder blown across my path, a greater dis-ease of emotional fear came from the pictures in my habitually agitated mind – ruminating perceptions about enactments that echoed as a voice in my head "not being good enough". This manifests in a painful and crushing unfulfilled need for belonging. If being on the outside looking in, or perhaps not even knowing where to look connects with you, I am by your side. I feel you.

Then, COVID-19 hit. Life and death became amplified in academia and beyond. Fortunately, I had already begun the process of releasing images and associated emotions that had taken me to the root of my habitual behaviours. Helpers at the Brooklyn Mediation Centre were my guides in becoming more aware of being present. I began to re-envision what it means to show up and embody life, moment to moment. In pausing to allow non-judgemental presence, I began to reclaim and piece together a broken self, discarding ego and reconnecting with the softer more vulnerable edges of my experience – integral to Thich Nhất Hạnh's (2010) discovering the magic of presence in being here. My mindfulness practice became an essential tool to reset and relate.

During COVID-19, my meditation practice evolved. I regularly enjoyed Brooklyn Meditation Centre's online programs including "Better Sleep Meditation". As vaccination became available, I rode my bike across Brooklyn's

"It be's that way sometime" 19

Image 2.1 "Journeying towards wholeness" illustration by Dean Noble.

Prospect Park to sit socially distanced in nature and meditate with members of the centre and curious passers-by. Through connection in the community, I felt held and at peace with myself. In turn, becoming more than ever committed to my purpose in life as a teacher educator, coteaching college classes, and a full-time NYC public high school teacher, publishing and presenting at virtual conferences.

A serendipitous circumstance, it is 11 pm ET as I write. My phone distracts with a humming text inquiry about an early morning meditation session! The line between my personal and professional mindfulness practice continues to blur. Even when my high school students were in remote learning, from my living room I passionately planned and facilitated a weekly zoom gathering of the Mindful Ambassadors student club with family members in tow for a guided meditation, inspirational videos, and music with representation that both recognised and celebrated the diversity of our collective. As a result of my daily meditation at home and in virtual/physical classrooms with my students, I am grateful for being released from expectations and my inner fears to see "what-is". With each healing breath I invite my emotions to flow without resistance, shame, or self-harm, opening for empathic connection and building the capacity to be present for compassionate care, essential to our mutual liberation.

20 Linda Noble with Malgorzata Powietrzynska

Transcending space and time towards connection: Malgorzata's story

It's February 14, 2019 at JFK airport. I board a LOT Airline Dreamliner bound for Poland. I'm elated at the prospect of spending the next two weeks with my family "back home". My semi-annual visits have become an important self-care ritual at whose core is reconnecting by being with the loved ones from whom I separated when I immigrated to the United States more than 30 years ago. As always, our blissful time together passes by too quickly. When I cross the Atlantic on my way back to what has become my home away from home, I reminisce about the moments of togetherness. At the same time, I am troubled by the reports of the rising COVID-19 cases in Western Europe. Indeed, by March 13, Europe is declared by the World Health Organisation as the epicentre of the pandemic (Nebehay, 2020) with Italy becoming the first country worldwide to introduce a national lockdown.

Tragically, New York is not far behind as it begins to register terrifying rates of infections, hospitalisations, and deaths. Within two short weeks following my return flight, which was filled with maskless travellers, I found myself experiencing COVID-19-like symptoms. My doctor, who has no tools to diagnose the condition (at the time, testing is restricted to individuals in need of hospitalisation), advises me to stay home and monitor my symptoms. Amid an emotional avalanche of helplessness and uncertainty, fear sets in. My mental and physical wellbeing are off-balance and in an urgent need of self-generated care. Thus, I resort to the intergenerational healing wisdom of my ancestors (Powietrzynska et al., 2015), the tried-and-true home remedies, such as frequent gargling with salt water, drinking honey and lemon, and simply resting in bed. I also apply what I have learned from local friends who practise complementary medicine including Jin Shin Jyutsu flows and holds and herbalism (Powietrzynska, 2017). As I slowly return to a healthy equilibrium, the city starts to shut down and the university system I work for engages (at an unprecedented speed) in the transition to remote work.

Notwithstanding the surrounding circumstances of COVID-19-induced suffering being experienced by many, to me, most of what came with the pivot to working from home was a welcome change. Absent was the daily two-hour sentence to crawl to-and-from work in the thick of the New York traffic. Abandonment of long-haul driving paved the way to strolling the suddenly quiet and peaceful local streets while breathing the air that got fresher and cleaner, hearing chirping of the birds, and finally being able to explore together the residential neighbourhood that had hosted my partner Alex and I for several years. The five-minute "commute" between the bedroom and my home-based office space afforded extended sleep, whose well-documented benefits for mental and physical health are often underappreciated and undervalued (Huffington, 2017). More time at home created space for Alex and I to enjoy each other's company in creating and savouring healthy, nutritious home-cooked meals that replaced the often hurried, grab-'n-go, gobbled-up-in-isolation foods of our pre-pandemic fast-paced, too-busy, and time-famished lives. Without much notice, we became recipients of a gift of time, which, according to Ashley Whillans (2020) who refers to herself as a happiness researcher, is our most valuable resource. Based in Harvard Business School, Whillans' research unequivocally and unapologetically demonstrates that making time to engage in happiness producing activities (i.e., "time affluence") is essential to human flourishing. For me, gardening the small plot in the back of our house was among such joy-creating activities. I was able to tend to and enjoy my plants on a daily basis and, together with Alex, we cherished the moments outdoors in our tiny sliver of nature.

Importantly, remote work removed the rigidity of spatial boundaries that often tie us down to what we may perceive as undesirable physical environments (such as crowded, noisy, and poorly lit or ventilated office spaces). The built environment has been found to have both direct and indirect effects on mental health (Evans, 2003). As noted by Evans (2003), restoration (e.g., recovery from cognitive fatigue and stress) is one of the indirect mental health correlates of the built environment. Thanks to my relatively privileged social positionality, I was fortunate to be able to leave the city for extended periods of time to work from and enjoy the tranquillity of my friends' house in a small oceanside town. While there, I supported my wellness by indulging in long walks along the deserted beaches while watching and listening to the ever-present whispers or roars of ocean waves spilling onto the sandy shores. I took solace in observing the industrious sanderlings scuttling back and forth in a perpetual "wave chase" sand-dipping their tiny beaks in search of nourishment blissfully unaware of the grave existential threat being faced by their fellow (human) species. Evans (2003) remarks that exposure to natural elements such as trees, water, and natural landscapes has been shown to replenish cognitive energy.

Counterintuitively, the need to maintain a physical distance afforded more frequent and perhaps deeper connections with my co-workers who, like me, appeared to enjoy an expanded spatial and temporal flexibility. Having adopted the marvels of video-conferencing technologies, many of us found ourselves a few mouse clicks away from each other. Given the paralysing uncertainty and emotional toll associated with the fast-developing, seemingly all-engulfing pandemic, my very first managerial instinct was to reach out to my colleagues with genuine curiosity and care. To that end, I took time to virtually connect with each of my academic co-workers, asking how they were REALLY doing and how I could be of assistance. Oftentimes, all that was needed was my being fully present and engaging in mindful listening by paying attention and withholding judgement (Kabat-Zinn, 1994). Indeed, Cortland Dahl and colleagues (2020) point out that connection (framed as a subjective sense of care and kinship toward other people) promotes supportive relationships and caring interactions. Furthermore, they argue that connection and attention together with insight and purpose in life are the core pillars of our mental wellbeing which, at a neural level, show a quality of plasticity or trainability (Dahl et al., 2020).

22 Linda Noble with Malgorzata Powietrzynska

Regardless of the modality (physical or virtual), when we come together, we do so in what we think of as space. Doreen Massey conceptualises space as the product of interrelations, the sphere of coexisting heterogeneity and multiplicity, always under construction and never closed (Rose, 2007). In that sense, space is not static or immobile. According to Massey (2003), arrival is not landing in an awaiting passive destination but an intertwining of ongoing trajectories (of those entering and those who may be occupying the space entered). When moving from one place to another, we travel not across space-as-surface but across a multitude of ongoing stories. In this movement of process and change, we must recognise that space necessarily intersects with time (Massey, 2003).

The fields of positive psychology and neuroscience offer mounting scientific evidence that social connection and spending quality time with others matters for our flourishing. Sliding down from our heads to our hearts affords the felt sense of such, finding the proverbial proof in the pudding. Since maintaining close ties has over the years been a source of strength supporting my family through thick and thin, the time of COVID-19 could have been no exception. Indeed, it became an opportunity to defy the limitations imposed by the always-too-short-three-week-annual-time-allotments and to spend more time together. And so, in the two years of the pandemic, having crossed the big pond a few times, I enjoyed months of daily living with those who I care most about.

Social connection and our flourishing

In mindfully being together, we (Malgorzata and Linda) consistently reflect upon our perceptions about feeling fragmented and becoming whole. This approach allows for our true nature and authentic presence to evolve. Self-awareness (Davidson & Begley, 2012) and transparency in our relationship affirms our sense of belonging. In this section, we celebrate how empathic curiosity (Brown, 2012) and compassion (Neff, 2003), rather than critical judgement, water the seeds of our growing connection to each other.

The entwined nature of our relationship is reflected in the mirror of what Tara Brach (2020) refers to as RAIN, recognising through self-awareness the humanity within. RAIN is an acronym describing the meditation practice that supports development of radical compassion.

> R = *recognising* what's happening right here
> A = *allowing* to let be for right now, to not fix, or judge or ignore
> I = *investigating* or bringing a curious attention to what's here
> N = *nurturing* or getting in touch with vulnerability

Brach (2020) reminds us that *nurturing* dissolves the sense of a scared separated self and allows us to feel the kind of belonging that frees us up from the grip

"It be's that way sometime" 23

Image 2.2 Savouring life's gifts.

of fear because fear is the perception of separation . . . loss of connectedness especially during difficult times. Thus, through RAIN we each found a way to abandon fearful fragmentation and to not only cultivate a wholesome sense of compassion for ourselves (as described in our respective self-care stories told earlier) but also to continue to attune to love (Salzberg, 2017) and compassionate presence to each other.

We have over time poured a cup of trust for each other from which to sip and pause. On occasion, one can with comfort "step back" while sensing the other "lean in" and unconditionally welcome our "guests". The "guests" in these teachable moments of presence are emotions of life that arrive into a consciously co-created space. In this open space, our mutual curiosity fosters a climate that supports our bearing risk across a bridge of fear and personal vulnerability (Brown, 2012) to savour the collective fruits of compassionate growth. Stepping back in our case literally meant that when I (Malgorzata) was thousands of miles away in Poland, my being present in class transcended the concept of time and space thanks to the flexibility and resilience (Davidson & Begley, 2012) Linda and I had already established prior to the pandemic. Simultaneously, I (Linda) experienced a sense of loss in not being able to travel and physically be with my family in Ireland. Malgorzata and I coming together in planning and teaching helped in alleviating the pain I felt in being isolated from the ones I love.

At the same time, I (Linda) was riding a roller coaster as my son weaved through the harrowing college application process. On more than one occasion, Malgorzata intuitively took the reins for the SEL opening (Jagers et al., 2021) while I found my grounding and sat silently orienting myself, preparing to meet the needs of the upcoming remote class as well as the expectations of the group. Similarly, in a reciprocal nature Linda stepped forward as an instrument of attunement when I (Malgorzata) experienced connectivity issues logging in from afar. Yet, our intention was at all times to keep our students aware of challenges we were experiencing individually or together, modelling mindful coping skills in the face of adversity. In releasing myself from the guise of a superhero, I (Linda) frequently shared in class my feelings about being consumed by the trials and tribulations striving to raise a teenage boy in NYC and how a few laps in the local public swimming pool helped me to unplug and clear my mind. Consistency in my formal practice was the rudder through storms of emotion while I was also sustained by anchoring my moment-to-moment attention in applied practice. Each type of practice informed the other. Overall, my circumstances remain unchanged yet my mindset shifts to one of gratitude. In these moments of fractured presence shared above, we had opportunities to practise for ourselves and mirror for each other strategies that were both liberating and inviting of the quality of attention that comes from holistic presence. On occasion we welcomed a more than human presence as cats, dogs, and hamsters graced our screens with their casual curiosity and lively spontaneity.

We mined valuable resources of emotional strength from our partnership. As noted by psychologist Roy Baumeister and his colleagues (2007), scientists have placed emotion at the centre of wisdom pointing to the contribution of emotion to clear thinking. For us the enactment of RAIN served as a mindful practice for everyday living and transformation. Beyond tolerance, we celebrated and integrated complementary aspects of our intellectual, sensing, and feeling selves. This manifested in how we both observed rather than controlled in *Recognising* and openly accepting in *Allowing* each other's authentic presence as well as how we compassionately *Investigated* and *Nurtured* our aspiration to enact an equity focused pedagogy (Powietrzynska et al., 2021). Grounded in our humanity of interbeing (Nhất Hạnh, 2017), we extended this web of connection in our mindful practice of engagement with the communities for which we are blessed to serve. In the next section, we describe how we grew in our contemplative approach with wellbeing.

M.E.L.T. and a pedagogy of human experience

Two years prior to the onset of the COVID-19 pandemic, encouraged by like-minded colleagues, we realised our vision to develop a college course, fondly named M.E.L.T. (Mindfulness for Everyday Living and Transformation). Upon its inception, our baby was rejected by the all-male general education committee. Deprived of this paternal adoption, the course gained insufficient enrolment despite the tenacity and good faith of a department chair who placed it in the cradle of a college course catalogue semester after semester. Fortuitously, during the height of the pandemic, an opportunity opened up to breathe life into the course. In Spring 2021, a director of one of the college's educational opportunity programs recognised the course's potential. The dust was blown off the syllabus, which until that moment had been relegated to a shelf of academia misfits.

M.E.L.T.'s target freshman cohort had been identified as being in need of compassionate pedagogical support. These resilient individuals showed promise transitioning into a rigorous college environment despite their prior academic records that had been compromised by circumstances often beyond their control. The program director and counsellor shared an aspiration to cultivate students' sense of belonging, through implicit mindful attunement and explicit trauma sensitive coping strategies that enhance wellbeing. They believed that the M.E.L.T. curriculum shepherded by our coteaching partnership and contemplative pedagogy grounded in social justice and compassion (Noble & Powietrzynska, 2021) presented a unique and timely intervention for their students. Given the green light, we were elated to move forward while naive about the challenges that lay ahead and the deep gratitude we would owe to our students for the journey we were supported in navigating together. In the upcoming sections, an opening student quote grounds our narrative.

What does it mean to show up?

> One thing I learned for me would be that I am now more vocal on how I feel and I feel the need to keep this up.

The education we (Malgorzata and Linda) received was humbling and essential as we grew together in our humanity. Our students taught us a new definition of presence as they advocated for cameras being off when eating, after a long day of work, an extensive commute, or breastfeeding a child. The relationship we built together was less bending and more flexing especially in a virtual classroom during COVID-19. At the same time, we learned to value our aspirational ideal dispositions, "being here, being kind" or "seeking the common good". At the opening of each class session, we collectively invoked these intentions. We (Malgorzata and Linda) struggled with how to invite our students' spirits in the *ubuntu* sense (Oviawe, 2016) recognising the inequity of circumstance in which we individually exist. A teachable moment emerged when a student who became the spokesperson for the group during one of our initial class sessions challenged our insistence that cameras be on. This student – our teacher – helped us understand the naivety of our asking and the harsh nature of our insistence especially during an in-class autobiography assignment for which students were to free-write "All about Me". Blinded by our privilege, we were mindless in demanding that students "bear all" on camera and heartless in how removed we positioned ourselves from their lived experience in that moment. When stopped in our tracks, we felt nagging shame, the need to own our actions and the unintentional harm. We were deeply grateful to the cohort who listened and welcomed us back as we embraced an understanding of presence that was emergent and contingent (Tobin & Ritchie, 2012).

Finding our rhythm

> I started good, but now that I have a job and more responsibilities, I have trouble keeping up with this class and my other classes.

In calling for "a hard re-set" demanded by COVID-19 and anti-Black pandemics of 2020, Gloria Ladson-Billings (2021) advocates engagement in culturally relevant pedagogy that takes into account the conditions of students' lives these occurrences set in motion. Initially, in our enactment of what we understand to be a culturally relevant pedagogy, we were guided by intuition and trust. Narelle Lemon & Sharon McDonough (2021) note, "it is the embracing of uncertainty that allows the cultivation of intuition and trust, a letting go of what we have become familiar with and opening up to finding a way, new ways that embrace wholeheartedness" (p. 11). It wasn't until sometime later that we were introduced to Joe Feldman's (2019) concept of grading for equity. Indeed, we decided to take a stronger stance in our role as educators in adapting our social justice pedagogy by listening to students' pleas to reduce and/ or eliminate the burden of *home*work. For many of our students "home" is an aspiration – a fluid concept. There was tension between this context and their identities as fledgling academics. For some, a trip to a grandmother's apartment to access a computer meant college assignments got done. For others, childcare negated any opportunity to sit in reflection beyond class time. This necessitated our developing and providing scaffolds on which student dyads/triads might land on during class, a set of benchmarks from which they might self-assess and envision the climb ahead. The scaffolds took the form of a guided reading practice, checklists, graphic organisers, time tables, and "to do" lists, each providing transparency essential in our journey together. The purpose was to address what can be crippling – a sense of overwhelm or inadequacy as well as an intention to not leave anyone behind as we aspired to support grit (Duckworth, 2016) and growth mindset (Dweck, 2017). The trail was collectively bushwhacked as we proceeded. We (Malgorzata and Linda) placed in our back pockets the vestiges of guide hats. Instead, with sharpened pencils we took careful note of the steps taken in traversing the unknown territory of humanity which we shared. We were awestruck by the MWe (Siegel, 2014) in dynamic situations and unforeseen events recorded. As we travelled, we each grew closer to and more settled in the home within.

Authors and readers connect

> I think the guest speakers are a plus. I loved them, especially when we were learning about alzheimers.

The move to remote learning afforded bringing into our collective Zoom space a few authors of texts that we were exploring in the course. We considered the presence of our invited colleagues as a way to break down the ivory tower by humanising the textual experience beyond it being an act of reading and talking about what some faceless "academic experts" wrote. This approach was consistent with Ladson-Billings' (2021) call for a shift towards culturally relevant pedagogy which requires a move beyond lectures and telling as teaching. The authors of assigned readings emerged as people with hearts and souls with whom our students were able to connect. Indeed, in preparing for a visit, we agreed with our authors that creating an experience of mindful engagement and connection would be our collective goal. To that end, we strove towards modelling how to shift academia's prioritised cognitive processing of theoretical concepts into what we aspired to – a felt experience of their practical applications. In other words, we were bringing the authors into the class to allow us to viscerally connect with them in a space mediated by our shared understanding of the work. Through this approach, in a tradition of authentic inquiry (Alexakos, 2015), we courageously explored how what we were learning was indeed relevant and might benefit each of us as individuals and as a community during this time of COVID-19-induced mind- and heartache.

We were astonished by the relative ease with which kindness bubbled up in each of the "guest-led" sessions. For example, Cristina Trowbridge's work in the Museum of Natural History (2017) came alive as she engaged our group in an exercise of sketching dioramas. Through demonstrating how, as we draw, our respective attention and focus may go to different places, Cristina brought to light a notion of polysemia (Tobin, 2009) and the beauty and strength that

28 Linda Noble with Malgorzata Powietrzynska

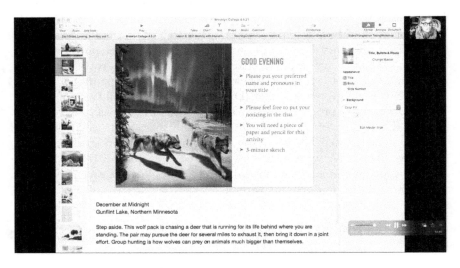

Image 2.3 Sketching a diorama with Cristina.

may emanate from the openness to the multitude of perceptions and perspectives. We were also gifted with potentially healing moments of silence during contemplative sketching acts of focused attention.

Another guest, Kenneth Tobin, whose work is driven by an imperative to expand and deepen functional literacy in wellness as part of a necessary education, joined us from his retirement home in Florida. Ken shared examples of self-help practices that allow individuals to be autonomous and proactive in avoiding sickness and directly addressing symptoms as necessary. For example, Ken brought to our attention the importance of nasal rather than oral inhalation and exhalation. Together, we engaged in a short breathing meditation accompanied by humming on the outbreath – a mindful practice which research suggests considerably increases the amount of nitric oxide transferred to the airways (Tobin & Alexakos, 2021). In addition, being with Ken heightened our sense of the mind-body connection and brought joy to our session as pictured below (Image 2.4). By practising simple Jin Shin Jyutsu finger holds/mudras (Tobin, 2017), we learned how to ameliorate with compassion potentially deleterious emotions like anger and fear.

Perhaps the most impactful and/or memorable virtual visit (as evidenced in the opening student quote) was that by Amy Goods who introduced our collective to her work on play (Goods, 2016). Amy's conceptualisation of play is based in "connectivity, inner-personal reciprocity of care, love, and compassion for the other" (Goods, 2016, p. 263). Indeed, Amy's presence was an embodiment of these very qualities as she gently connected with our collective by finding ways to make her story relevant to ours (i.e., having a memory-loss-inflicted

Image 2.4 Enjoying mudras with Ken.

family member), showing a genuine interest in us as individuals (i.e., asking what we do for play), or bringing her own child into our space. Each of our guests was a teacher in a pedagogy of common human experience as they demonstrated unique approaches to creating a sense of togetherness.

Self-care is not selfish

> This class is like a nice reminder of how what i go through is fine and normal and how i should take my time and to do what i need in order to get better.

In the quote above, the student invokes a concept of self-compassion which is an expression of a healthy attitude in relationship to oneself. Kristin Neff (2003) notes that self-compassion "involves being touched by and open to one's own suffering, not avoiding or disconnecting from it, generating the desire to alleviate one's suffering and to heal oneself with kindness" as well as "offering non-judgemental understanding to one's pain, inadequacies and failures, so that one's experience is seen as part of the larger human experience" (p. 87). The student's "inner wisdom" is evident in her statement that the class was a "nice reminder" about the gamut of emotions we experience. She articulates a connection between her self-awareness and the vast pool of emotions we welcomed in our relationships to each other. The burden of conforming to a critique of "acceptable normal experience" was relieved by students' deepening connection to an inner sense of flow by allowing what was present to just be. Simultaneously, overtime, our collective became connected by avoiding getting stuck in "me" versus "them" or alternate self-absorbed forms of othering. The commitment to regularly embrace ideal dispositions as noted earlier, was a precursor for creating a safe and courageous space to accommodate an authentic sense of belonging in community by seeking common ground.

Ending with gratitude

We (Malgorzata and Linda) face a new challenge to mindfully reset and attune to the traumatic remnants of a post-COVID-19 reality. This requires gazing beyond the self, beyond judgements of circumstance and mortal desires to instead connect and embrace the nature of our MWe – being as one. We are grounded in teaching/learning about the relevance and power mediated by authentic connection, being both vulnerable and courageous in compassionate relationship toward self/other. Living with gratitude we continue to learn, finding comfort and joy in connection and in building relationships.

We invite you to lean into this practice. My friend, come by and visit again. Meantime, we wish for you to live mindfully, we wish for you to embrace patience and gratitude. Together in becoming liberated, may we coexist by caring for our mutual wellbeing entwined with the health of our planet, the home we share.

References

Alexakos, K. (2015). *Being a teacher/researcher: A primer on doing authentic inquiry research on teaching and learning.* Sense Publishers.

Baumeister, R. F., Vohs, K. D., Nathan DeWall, C., & Zhang, L. (2007). How emotion shapes behaviour: Feedback, anticipation, and reflection, rather than direct causation. *Personality and Social Psychology Review, 11*(2), 167–203. https://doi.org/10.1177/1088868307301033

Brach, T. (2004). *Radical acceptance: Embracing your life with the heart of a Buddha.* Bantam Books.

Brach, T. (2020). Radical compassion in challenging times. *Psychotherapy Networker.* www.psychotherapynetworker.org/magazine/toc/187/where-are-we-going

Brown, B. (2012). *Daring greatly: How the courage to be vulnerable transforms the way we live, love, parent, and lead.* Gotham Books.

Dahl, C. J., Wilson-Mendenhall, C. D., & Davidson, R. J. (2020). The plasticity of wellbeing: A training-based framework for the cultivation of human flourishing. *Proceedings of the National Academy of Science, 117*(51). https://doi.org/10.1073/pnas.2014859117

Davidson, R., & Begley, S. (2012). *The emotional life of your brain: How its unique patterns affect the way you think, feel, and live – and how you can change them.* Hudson Street Press.

Duckworth, A. L. (2016). *Grit: The power of passion and perseverance.* Scribner Book Company.

Dweck, C. (2017). *Mindset – updated edition: Changing the way you think to fulfil your potential.* Little, Brown Book Group.

Ergas, O. (2017). *Reconstructing "education" through mindful attention: Positioning the mind at the centre of curriculum and pedagogy.* Palgrave Macmillan.

Evans, W. V. (2003). The built environment and mental health. *Journal of Urban Health: Bulletin of the New York Academy of Medicine, 80*(4), 536–555. https://doi.org/10.1093/jurban/jtg063

Feldman, J. (2019). *Grading for equity: What it is, why it matters, and how it can transform schools and classrooms.* Corwin, a SAGE Company

Goods, A. (2016). The possibility of play: Understanding the transformative nature of play and exploring the possible applications for people with Alzheimer's. In M. Powietrzynska & K. Tobin (Eds.), *Mindfulness and educating citizens for everyday life* (pp. 258–269). SensePublishers.

Hammond, Z. (2021). *Liberatory education: Integrating the science of learning and culturally responsive practice*. American Educator. www.aft.org/ae/summer2021/hammond.

Huffington, A. S. (2017). *The sleep revolution: Transforming your life, one night at a time*. Harmony Books.

Jagers, R. J., Rivas-Drake, D., & Williams, B. (2019). Transformative social and emotional learning (SEL): Toward SEL in service of educational equity and excellence. *Educational Psychologist, 54*(3), 162–184. https://doi.org/10.1080/00461520.2019.1623032

Jagers, R. J., Skoog-Hoffman, A., Barthelus, B., & Schlund, J. (2021). *Transformative social and emotional learning: In pursuit of educational equity and excellence*. American Educator.

Kabat-Zinn, J. (1994). *Wherever you go, there you are: Mindfulness meditation in everyday life*. Hyperion.

Koffman, J. P. (2012). *To see the truth: The teachings of venerable Pramote Pamojjo*. Suan Santidham.

Ladson-Billings, G. (2021). I'm here for the hard res-set: Post pandemic pedagogy to preserve our culture. *Equity & Excellence in Education, 54*(1), 68–78. https://doi.org/10.108 0/10665684.2020.1863883

Lemon, N. S., & McDonough, S. (2021). If not now, then when? Wellbeing and wholeheartedness in Education. *The Educational Forum, 85*(3), 317–335. https://doi.org/10.10 80/00131725.2021.1912231

Lorde, A. (1997). The uses of anger. *Women's Studies Quarterly, 25*(1/2), 278–285. www.jstor.org/stable/40005441

Luvmour, B. (2021). Commentary: Social justice and holistic education – A renewal. *Holistic Education Review, 1*(1).

Massey, D. (2003). Some times of space. In S. May (Ed.), *Olafur Eliasson: The weather project* (pp. 107–118). Tate Publishing.

Mind and Life Education Research Network. (2012). Contemplative practices and mental training: Prospects for American education. *Child Development Perspectives, 6*, 146–153. https://doi.org/10.1111/j.1750-8606.2012.00240.x

Mpamira-Kaguri, T. (2019, November). *Trauma not transformed is trauma transferred* [Video]. TEDxOakland. www.ted.com/talks/tabitha_mpamira_kaguri_trauma_not_transformed_is_trauma_transferred_what_baton_are_you_passing_on

Nebehay, S. (2020, March 13). Europe is epicenter of the coronavirus pandemic: WHO. *Reuters*. Retrieved 8 May 2021.

Neff, K. (2003). Self-compassion: An alternative conceptualization of a healthy attitude toward oneself. *Self and Identity, 2*(2), 85–101. https://doi.org/10.1080/15298860309032

Nhất Hạnh, T. (2010). *You are here: Discovering the magic of the present moment*. Shambhala Publications, Inc.

Nhất Hạnh, T. (2017). *The art of living: Peace and freedom in the here and now*. HarperCollins Publishers.

Noble, L., & Powietrzynska, M. (2021). Bushwhacking a path forward: Contemplative pedagogy for wellbeing in education. In N. Lemon (Ed.), *Creating a place for self-care and wellbeing in higher education: Finding meaning across academia* (pp. 147–158). Routledge.

Oviawe, J. (2016). How to rediscover the *ubuntu* paradigm in education. *International Review of Education, 62*, 1–10. https://doi.org/10.1007/s11159-016-9545-x

Palmer, P. (2004). *A hidden wholeness: The journey toward an undivided life*. John Wiley & Sons, Inc.

Powietrzynska, M. (2017). Taking charge of our own wellness through complementary approaches. In M. Powietrzynska & K. Tobin (Eds.), *Weaving complementary knowledge systems and mindfulness to educate a literate citizenry for sustainable and healthy lives* (pp. 65–81). SensePublishers. https://doi.org/10.1007/9789463511827_021

Powietrzynska, M., Noble, L., O'Loughlin-Boncamper, S., & Azeez, A. (2021). Holding space for uncertainty and vulnerability: Reclaiming humanity in teacher education through contemplative | equity pedagogy. *Cultural Studies of Science Education, 16*, 951–964. https://doi.org/10.1007/s11422-021-10035-x

Powietrzynska, M., Tobin, K., & Alexakos, K. (2015). Facing the grand challenges through heuristics and mindfulness. *Cultural Studies of Science Education, 10*, 65–81. https://doi.org/10.1007/s11422-014-9588-x

Rose, G. (2007). For space – by Doreen Massey. *Geographical Research, 45*(2), 205–207. https://doi.org/10.1111/j.1745-5871.2007.00452.x

Salzberg, S. (2017, June 22). *Real love: The art of mindful connection* \ *Talks at Google* [Video file].

Siegel, D. (2014, February 28). The self is not defined by the boundaries of our skin. The mind is not only embodied but shaped by our relationships as well. *Psychology Today*.

Simmons, D. (2016). Impostor syndrome, a reparative history. *Engaging Science, Technology, and Society, 2*, 106–125. https://doi.org/10.17351/ests2016.33

Stark, C. A. (2019). Gaslighting, misogyny, and psychological oppression. *The Monist, 102*(2), 221–235. https://doi.org/10.1093/monist/onz007

Tobin, K. (2009). Connecting science education to a world in crisis. *Asia Pacific Science Education, 1*, 2. https://doi.org/10.1186/s41029-015-0003-z

Tobin, K. (2015). The sociocultural turn in science education and its transformative potential. In C. Milne, K. Tobin, & D. DeGennaro (Eds.), *Sociocultural studies and implications for science education* (pp. 3–31). Springer. https://doi.org/10.1007/978-94-007-4240-6_1

Tobin, K. (2017). Researching mindfulness and wellness. In M. Powietrzynska & K. Tobin (Eds.), *Weaving complementary knowledge systems and mindfulness to educate a literate citizenry for sustainable and healthy lives* (pp. 1–18). SensePublishers. https://doi.org/10.1007/9789463511827_002

Tobin, K., & Alexakos, K. (2021). Global challenges need attention now: Educating humanity for wellness and sustainability. *Cultural Studies of Science Education, 16*, 651–673. https://doi.org/10.1007/s11422-021-10080-6

Tobin, K., & Ritchie, S. M. (2012). Multi-method, multi-theoretical, multi-level research in the learning sciences. *Asia-Pacific Education Researcher, 21*(1), 117–129.

Trowbridge, C. A. (2017). Drawing attention: Notes from the field. In M. Powietrzynska & K. Tobin (Eds.), *Weaving complementary knowledge systems and mindfulness to educate a literate citizenry for sustainable and healthy lives* (pp. 171–183). SensePublishers. https://doi.org/10.1007/978-94-6351-182-7_12

Van der Kolk, B. (2015). *The body keeps the score*. Penguin Books.

Wall, S. (2006). An autoethnography on learning about autoethnography. *International Journal of Qualitative Methods, 5*(2), 146–160. https://doi.org/10.1177/160940690600500205

Whillans, A. (2020). *Time smart: How to reclaim your time and live a happier life*. Harvard Business Review Press.

3   Generating the place of self-compassion in higher education

An academic place of belonging as a catalyst of the COVID-19 pandemic

Narelle Lemon and Joanna Higgins

Introduction

The pandemic has revealed the need to position compassion and (self-)care at the heart of what we do as educators, leaders, and researchers, and for the students we work with in higher education. Revealed for us as research collaborators has been the place of belonging, from the perspective of how we create and sustain meaningful connections. From a strengths based view, we have seen the coronavirus or COVID-19 as it is commonly referred to and the changes that have emerged to how we work as academics as providing opportunities amongst a sad situation that the pandemic has created. For us, two women working in academia, one located in Australia and the other in New Zealand, we have found we have been able to connect more, reflect with each other, and embrace a common humanity that has enabled the harnessing of kindness, deep thinking, and expression of authentic self. We have pushed ourselves cognitively in partnership with taking moments to express what it has been like to live through lockdowns, uncertainties, social distancing, community anxiety, and local, global, and international unknowns. "Building and preserving positive social relations through scholarly exchanges" (Siry, 2021, pp. 320–321) has been key to generating care and self-compassion for ourselves, each other, our colleagues, and the scholarly work we undertake. This embodiment has supported and developed our sense of belonging.

We draw on a metalogue emergent methodology in this chapter (Roth & Tobin, 2004). We reconstruct our understanding of working together at this time of the pandemic, and thus the meaningful connection that has been sustained and extended. Collective memory and collective theorising is shared through our sharing of lived experience. The process has allowed us to embody an understanding of self with the journey being "mutual and reciprocal" (Norris & Sawyer, 2012, p. 13). What is significant about metaloguing as a reflexive form of writing is that from collective remembering in which the "voices of participants endure on their own rather than disappearing in the voice of a collective author" (Roth & Tobin, 2004, p. 1) comes the integration of compassion, self-compassion, and belonging.

DOI: 10.4324/9781003315797-4

As academics located in two different countries, Australia and New Zealand, we acknowledge the different contexts associated with the impact of COVID-19 alongside the importance of placing self-compassion and belonging as central to how we support ourselves and each other. We draw on holistic education including mindfulness and wellbeing science to ponder, expose, and integrate moments of tension that highlight what belonging is, and can be, experienced particularly in relation to collaboration. Using ourselves as the research site, we compare and contrast our experiences through the exchange of written reflections. We juxtapose our texts and visual narratives to present a comparison of our experiences as we focus on belonging, care, self-care, and self-compassion as the main events during a time of change globally and for higher education. We problematise and trouble the dominant culture in higher education where we are competitive and the structures honour hierarchy, power and deficit ways of thinking or othering (Clegg, 2009) verses collegiality, co-learning, kindness, and mutual respect (Jarden & Jarden, 2022; Lemon, 2022) that embraces "collegial advocacy" (Lea & Stierer, 2009). As such, we (re)connect with the humanising perspective of care (Gay, 2018; Keeling, 2014; Mortari, 2016; Noddings, 2003) and see the pandemic as a catalyst for caring for self and one another as crucial. In this way we are positioning our individual, collective, and systematic conversations about wellbeing as integral to who we are (Lemon & McDonough, 2021).

Metalogue and collective remembering

As we share our narratives in the form of a metalogue and collective remembering we provide insights into how we came together as collaborators. Our work has intersected through the American Educational Research Association (AERA) conference and specifically the Holistic Education Special Interest Group (SIG). It is through this SIG we have been able to connect with each other's work and then form a collaboration that has resulted in multiple publications, international symposiums, and opportunities to form a research group where we provide constructive feedback on each other's work as well as our peers Malgorzata Powietrzynska and Linda Noble located in the United States of America, doctoral students Suskya Goodall and Grant Zouch located in New Zealand, and international colleagues Kenneth Tobin (USA), Suchitra Sarda (India/USA), Tabitha McKenzie (NZ), and Yau Yan Wong (Thailand). We began our collaboration face-to-face in New York in 2018, connecting after a round table presentation at AERA that led to proposing we should work together. As this collaboration formed the pandemic became the catalyst for us to become more comfortable with meeting virtually, utilising Zoom to extend out to Malgorzata, Linda, Suskya, and Grant with Ken, Tabitha, Suchitra, and Yau Yan joining us for specific projects. We moved from virtual mode and negotiating different time zones (sometimes up to four, with this being additional cognitive work), to virtually meeting every fortnight with an ease as if we were meeting in real life. The use of technology to connect about our work

Generating the place of self-compassion in higher education 35

and form bonds became synergistic. We write in Google Docs, and we meet regularly without seeing co-location as a boundary.

NARELLE: Much of the pandemic has been a blur for me. I say this from the perspective of the blurring of days, weeks, months, and years into each other. There have been some pivotal experiences however throughout the pandemic that are not a blur – especially my international collaborations where we have continued to meet virtually and be a source of motivation, inspiration and kindness.

In Melbourne we have had so many lockdowns. Breaking the record for the longest lockdown in the world with one at 111 days duration during July to October 2020. When I think about non-blur moments, it is the relationships I sustained and built throughout the pandemic that have been professionally and personally rewarding to humanise the pandemic, and how we can work as colleagues. My collaboration with Joanna and colleagues has been one of these moments.

JOANNA: In New Zealand there was largely gratitude for how our government handled the pandemic when it first hit our shores at the end of March; almost a collective sense of adventure and a reminder of earlier times when the country holidayed together over the Christmas holidays. I was lucky to be quickly able to set up my home work space complete with a large whiteboard on the end wall by my desk which has captured the essence of our ensuing collaborative projects. The shock of the first lockdown cemented our Wellington-based group's embrace of Google Docs and Zoom.

NARELLE: When the pandemic started, I was overseas leading a study tour and undertaking research in Malaysia and Singapore in January 2020. Flying out of Melbourne on the 1st January I, we really, had no idea what was about to hit us. By the time I was heading back home in late January, Singapore wasn't taking any risks. Masks were mandatory in public buildings and on public transport, hand sanitiser stations were at the front of every doorway you walked into, and there was an emergency health of international concern emerging. There was a level of uncertainty that none of us had experienced before. I flew home wearing a mask. That was so foreign at the time. Now, well that is a different story. Masks now accompany our wallet and keys as items we take everywhere with us. By March my home office was set up, on the kitchen island bench, with large butcher paper and sticky notes becoming my equivalent of my office whiteboard to track collaborations. And although I've moved homes three times, the butcher's paper and sticky notes still feature heavily on the wall behind me in virtual meetings.

JOANNA: I was in New York when I first heard about the pandemic. It was after I arrived in December 2019 and I did not know, but at that time the virus was already circulating in the city – which I read in news reports after I had returned to New Zealand. In fact, the last time I saw Malgorzata and

25 January 2020: The first case of novel coronavirus was confirmed by Victoria Health Authorities. The patient was a man from Wuhan, who flew to Melbourne from Guangdong on 19 January

30 January 2020: The World Health Organization declared the outbreak a 'Public Health Emergency of International Concern'

11 March 2020: The World Health Organization declared the outbreak a Pandemic

16 March 2020: Victoria declares a 'State of Emergency' (set to end after 4 weeks)

Restrictions imposed: 14-day isolation for all travellers entering Victoria; and, in line with national restrictions, no mass gatherings of more than 500 people moving forward and all cruise ships banned from docking at Australian ports

20 March 2020: As of 9pm, Australia closes its international borders to all but Australian Citizens, Permanent Residents and their immediate families including spouses, legal guardians, and dependants

23 March 2020: National Stage 1 Restrictions: From midday 23 March 2020, a national shutdown of pubs, clubs, hotels licenced premises, gyms, sporting venues, cinemas, casinos etc. was enforced to try and stop the spread of COVID throughout the country

26 March 2020: National Stage 2 Restrictions: From 26 March 2020 people were encouraged to stay at home unless it is necessary

30 March 2020, 11:59 pm: Lockdown 1 begins. Lockdown duration was 43 days

12 May 2020, 11:59 pm: Lockdown ends

29 June 2020: Vic Lockdown 1.5 (The Postcode Lockdown), requiring approximately 311,000 people to stay at home across 36 suburbs

8 July 2020, 11:59 pm: Lockdown 2 begins: 111 days

27 October 2020, 11:59 pm: Lockdown ends

12 February 2021, 11:59 pm: Victoria entered a snap 5-day called Lockdown 3

17 February 2021, 11:59 pm: Lockdown ends

21 April 2021, Victoria's first three mass vaccination centres were opened at the Melbourne Convention & Exhibition Centre, the Royal Exhibition Building in Carlton and in Geelong

27 May 2021, 11:59 pm: Lockdown 4 begins for 14 days

10 June 2021, 11:59 pm: Lockdown ends

15 July 2021, 11:59 pm: Lockdown 5 for 12 days

27 July 2021, 11:59 pm: Lockdown ends

5 August 2021, 8:00 pm: Lockdown 6 for 78 days

1 September 2021, during the Delta outbreak and Lockdown 6, the Victorian Government announced we were no longer aiming for COVID Zero, and so it stood to reason that case numbers would increase exponentially (like they had throughout the rest of the world)
The justification for the change in policy was the virility of the delta strain and the availability of vaccines, and that vaccinations were now the best way to get out of lockdown and live with COVID

13 October 2021, Victoria recorded 2,292 COVID cases – the highest number of cases in a day in the state and the country. During the Omicron surge, case numbers exploded again, recording 2,738 cases and 4 deaths

21 October 2021, 11:59 pm: Lockdown 6 ends

28 December 2021, rising sharply to 5,137 cases

Early January with daily case numbers surpassing the 20,000 mark, with 21,997 on **6 January 2022** and 21,728 on **7 January 2022** it becomes more common than not to know someone who has COVID

Image 3.1 Melbourne pandemic timeline [Photos from top 29 January 2000, Singapore; 27 August 2020, Parliament Station escalators, Melbourne; 29 July 2021, vaccination two; and 9 January 2022, Brunswick supermarket carpark Melbourne].

Image 3.2 New York adventures.

Linda was not long before I returned to New Zealand when we met on a snowy afternoon at The Rubin Museum of Art on W17th St in Manhattan to talk about our AERA 2020 symposium plans in the Holistic SIG with Narelle.

I don't remember having any pandemic anxiety or precautions associated with the trip back; in fact I had already booked for the next trip to New York for after AERA in San Francisco in April 2020. I was looking forward with excitement to being with first time conference goers, Grant and Suskya, and reconnecting with Narelle, Malgorzata, and Linda. The face-to-face meeting felt important as the next stage of consolidating collaborations with Narelle, Malgorzata, Linda, and the wider holistic education group.

NARELLE: Wow, both of us were overseas at the beginning of the pandemic. I flew 2nd February 2020. When did you fly home?

JOANNA: I flew on 20th January and arrived in New Zealand on 22nd January 2020.

NARELLE: We met in New York in 2018 at the Holistic Education Special Interest Group as part of the AERA.

JOANNA: I remember when I first met you – with gratitude to the universe and to trusting my instincts to trek across the Times Square neighborhood to find a final conference session so that I finished AERA 2018 on a high note. For me this had been a different experience to other AERAs as it was in my other "home", New York. I was staying in my usual 'hood, Long Island City, just across the East River from Manhattan in Queens. This meant that on the final day of the conference I was in no rush to check out of a hotel and catch a plane out of the city. AERA was being held across several Times Square hotels in my least favorite area of New York. The thought of getting out of this tourist zone and back to one of my favorite neighborhoods in Queens was top of mind. I'm so pleased that I pushed myself to find that last holistic SIG session of the conference and was rewarded with meeting Narelle and her colleagues, passionate holistic educators open and welcoming to newcomers such as me to their SIG.

NARELLE: I'm so glad you made the trek. I remember the large space we were in. A hall with tables, floorboards. There were about 14 of us huddled shoulder to shoulder together around two circular tables joined together so we could hear each other amongst multiple other table clusters doing the same. It was a session of roundtables, and for the session Joanna was a part of I was the discussant. And it was the last session of the day, with most people having already transitioned to the airport to fly home. It was the first time I really felt like I had found my "people". It was the first time being a part of the SIG for the full program for me, having met the Program Chairs the previous year and I was privileged to attend one session that had sparked my interest back in 2017.

JOANNA: Finding the holistic SIG was not of course completely random. My academic identity had been expanding from mathematics education to incorporate wellbeing and contemplative practices over two decades of trips to New York. During this time I had the opportunity to go to the City University of New York Graduate Centre where I was lucky to learn about wellbeing and wellness from Ken Tobin and in the process got to know Malgorzata and her colleague, Linda. Malgorzata, Linda, and I had talked about future AERA presentations but we didn't know which division or SIG to target a proposal. That afternoon, ironically in New York, the answer emerged! That sunny afternoon in early spring opened up a whole new world of academic possibilities for me and my colleagues arising from that chance walk across Times Square, navigating tourists, food trucks, and random street performers jostling for dollars. In hindsight I was so grateful not to be rushing to the airport that day, but instead taking a contemplative walk from 6th to 8th avenues to meet Narelle, a fellow Antipodean.

Generating the place of self-compassion in higher education 39

Images 3.3 and *3.4* The beginning of our collaboration at roundtable conversations (2018 AERA).

The holistic SIG members were welcoming with the convenors, Michelle and Jennifer, suggesting we submit a symposium for the next AERA, perhaps on international perspectives on wellbeing . . . that was

40 *Narelle Lemon and Joanna Higgins*

the beginning of our collaboration with Narelle. Over dinner post conference I was excited to tell Malgorzata and Linda about finding our "home" at the holistic SIG. We immediately made plans to develop the symposium proposal virtually with Narelle over May, June and early July 2019, when I was back in New Zealand.

NARELLE: And we have been collaborating ever since, including with our colleagues, Suskya, Grant, Malgorzata, and Linda. Each year making plans to propose a symposium that brings together our individual projects under a collective umbrella with the intention for our research to also then be published in other formats. But what the pandemic has gifted us is normalising virtual meetings.

Pre 2020 organising meetings across often three or four different time zones was onerous. The pandemic has changed this. It is just a part of our professional life. A joyous part of academic life where we have been able to collaborate with one another across multiple projects, three international conference symposiums, a special education journal where we formed an Asia-Pacific cluster of papers amongst a larger set, chapters for my edited series on wellbeing in higher education, and chapters for other editors where we have been able to form supportive critical friendship.

JOANNA: I first presented in a Holistic SIG roundtable on mindfulness in Toronto. Our colleagues Malgorzata and Linda were part of the same session chaired by Narelle; the beginnings of a very special collaboration.

Buoyed by the possibility of a "home" for a wellbeing-focused symposium, I invited my doctoral students and colleagues, Suskya and Grant, and colleague Tabitha to work with me on the NZ paper. In July 2019 we submitted the proposal to the AERA Holistic SIG and learned in November that we had been accepted to present in April 2020 in San Francisco. Alas, the many plans I had for navigating stimulating networks with my colleagues as first-timers to AERA were scuppered. I had imagined Suskya, Grant and Tabitha joining with me, not only in the formal scholarly sessions, but also in the chance brushes with "famous" people in the elevators, escalators, hallways and receptions to experience the "that's what they look like" moments for early career scholars. We had fully fleshed out funded plans for both Ken and Narelle to visit in the second half of 2020. Alas the pandemic had other plans! Unexpectedly what followed was a collaborative academic reset emerging out of our disappointments of the cancellation entirely of the 2020 AERA as the pandemic built up steam. I'm so pleased we made the decision to progress our collaboration using the structures of the AERA annual meeting and specifically our connectedness with and place of belonging in the Holistic SIG.

NARELLE: I'm thinking through the process of our collaboration and the outputs achieved. It is massive, and we have created a great community where we co-write, co-present, cite each other's work, and are editors and critical friends. In late 2019 we had our first symposium accepted for AERA 2020

Image 3.5 Connecting and reminiscing about AERA at the airport with colleagues.

with a focus on "International Perspectives on Embedding Generative Contemplative Practices to Enhance Wellbeing in Institutional Settings". But this conference was canceled as we all grappled with the pandemic and closing of international borders. We did however take our work from this unpresented symposium and each contributed to a special edition producing four papers for Cultural Studies of Science Education that was published in 2021 edited by Ken. Then in 2020 we generated our next symposium "Perspectives of International Citizen-Practitioners Respecting and Embracing Responsibility for Enhancing Holistic Wellbeing" for delivery at AERA 2021 knowing this would be virtual. At this conference we were also discussants and chairs of other panels for each other. And as we write this chapter our third symposium for AERA 2022 "Wellbeing and equity: An International focus on valuing humanity as education" will be presented in hybrid mode in April. Alongside this collective work I have had the pleasure of being a book series editor with Routledge on wellbeing and self-care in higher education and we have produced four book chapters across three different books in the series involving a different combination of co-authoring across 2021 and 2022. When I collate all we have achieved I'm so humbled to be working with amazing supportive colleagues who push me to continually extend my thinking in the space of wellbeing and holistic and contemplative practices. We really have been incredibly productive in supporting one another in connecting and sustaining our research group across various projects, and indeed across platforms. What I also appreciate is that we know each other's work so well that we can cross cite and build on knowledge and contribution to our research area.

JOANNA: An inspiring aspect of our collaboration is the ripple effect across our emerging and ever evolving group of colleagues interested in aspects of self-compassion in higher education. Suskya's and my work in appreciative circling and leadership has been cross pollinated in both directions by our research collaborations, both in ways of being as educators and scholars. Both your poetry, Narelle, and that of Malgorzata and Linda's sparked our interest in New Zealand in poeticising. We have explored this with Grant planning to include poeticising in his PhD and then in another project on initial teacher education work around emotions and maths with colleagues, Linda Bonne and Raewyn Eden, who were part of a Zoom call with you to talk about presenting data as poetic narratives. With borders opening up Narelle and I are now planning her visit to New Zealand to develop our collaboration across several projects. Our virtual working together has provided energy going forward.

NARELLE: We've been able to provide ourselves comfort as we have all pivoted in life during the pandemic. If someone can't make a meeting, we record the team meeting so it can be watched back later often with a message of "we missed you" shared. We write in Google Docs, a shared space that allows us to make comments to each other providing feedback on flow of ideas. We each read each other's writing, then come back together collectively to provide verbal feedback to strengthen our work individually and collectively. We have become a collaboration with heart showing up for each other holistically, spiritually, and cognitively. We laugh, check in, remember key moments, push one another, and have incredible respect. We have done this all virtually with a strength that cares for ourselves and each other.

JOANNA: The creation of a shared virtual space has been critical to building our scholarly community and building solidarity as a group. In this space we've been able to support each other through our developing scholarship. While some of us have met in person prior to the pandemic, others of us have got to know each other through reading each other's work alongside the opportunities to discuss what has been written and connect with related colleagues. The power of bringing ideas to life through a virtual platform should not be underestimated. It now means so much more to read a paper by our Australian and US colleagues. We know the subtexts underlying their ideas, resonating with their favorite turns of phrase which become our "short-hand" in further discussions. We hold dearly and celebrate the enduring sense of connectedness and belonging.

Generating the place of self-compassion in higher education 43

Image 3.6 The dynamics of our collaboration.

44 *Narelle Lemon and Joanna Higgins*

Image 3.7 Working virtually.

I see you there – time for a quick connect??? Hello, yes we can do that, Zoom. Yes ☺ I'll send a link via email.

Image 3.8 Screen conversations within text.

NARELLE: We have fostered meaningful connection in what has been unprecedented times, and when we know so many of our colleagues have felt isolated. We have to centre relationships, collaboration and support for one another. We have built structures that nurture scholarly coming together that embraces and embodies collective sharing of lived experiences of what it is to be an academic at this moment in time, resources. And we have a distributed leadership that honours perspective, open mindedness, and collegiality. We have cared for each other. Locating wellbeing centrally to how we work and what we work on. What stands out most significantly for me is that we embody a common humanity. We make time to listen and hold a grounded space for each other in life. Joanna in New Zealand, myself in Australia, and our other colleagues in the USA, India and Thailand have been living through a pandemic at the same time. That is true, however, each of us have had incredibly different experiences. We resonate. Sometimes we need to calm our self. Other times it is each other. We have been able to collectively navigate a kinship that allows for each of us to process and flourish no matter how long that takes. There is no anticipation of reward or recognition, rather we have the welfare of each other at the heart.

JOANNA: The google doc has become like a metaphorical open office door. Instead of physically walking to someone's office or calling out while writing we've connected virtually on the shared doc enabling not only a written conversation, but also a quick Zoom, particularly useful when working across time zones. To me this is not just an alternative, but an enhancement to belonging and connectedness that enriches our collaboration.

Coda

In taking an expansive approach we expand our metalogue and collective remembering to become a radical listener in exploring the experiences of being collaborators during a pandemic. Three themes emerge from our collaboration during the pandemic – self-compassion, care, and belonging.

Self-compassion

We are all connected to each other by the bonds we share, this our common humanity that allows us to embrace our imperfections, our vulnerabilities, and most importantly our ability to be aware of ourselves and each other with kindness. We make the choice to connect, share, and to learn from each other with an empathy whereby we bring compassion for each other, and self-compassion for ourselves. We come together to reflect upon, problem solve, and share insights into our local, national, and global perspectives.

We have made time to talk about what bonds us, this includes what makes us different. We listen deeply with open hearts and with a vulnerability to embrace how we can support one another. We have been able to collectively negotiate what it means to be an academic and researcher during a pandemic. We have negotiated what Siry (2021) notes as "challenges of uncertainty ushered in profound implications for the educational research community" (p. 319) together. This is where our vulnerability has been a beacon to help us realise our potential. We have been less hard on ourselves as we individually and collectively navigate the pandemic and the demands of what it means to be an academic or work in academia. By being self-compassionate we have been able to soften how we react to our inner dialogue, and support one another to still grow at a significant time of change and trauma. We have been able to catch ourselves in moments of self-criticism and talk through what it is we really want. We have given ourselves permission to experience feelings of loss or feelings of judgement while simultaneously encouraging each other to do things differently, to embrace working differently. We have been able to reframe the inner dialogues and become encouraging and supportive to ourselves and each other. Remembering as Kristne Neff says "that if you really want to motivate yourself, love is more powerful than fear" (Neff, 2011, p. 167).

Care

In higher education care, and especially self-care, has received little attention when it comes to how it can enhance the experiences for academics (Keeling, 2014; Lemon, 2021c; McKenzie & Blenkinsop, 2006). However, there is a rise with a focus on (self-)care and with this compassion, empathy, reciprocity, and how it can enhance relationships and a sense of belonging (Lemon, 2021a; Lemon & McDonough, 2018, 2021; Mckenzie & Blenkinsop, 2006).

With this comes a valuing of humanising the academy (Hall & Brault, 2021). For us care has been a throughline of our collaboration. We move between "I", "we", and "us" ways of working (Jarden & Jarden, 2022) that facilitates being authentic, caring for each other, ourselves, and the work we produce that honours the research we carry out. Care is central to our learning (Hay, 2019; Lemon, 2021b) and subsequent pedagogies embrace inclusion and the creation of human connections (Wolf, 2020). As such we are interrupting "time-honoured norms and routines, and [thus] . . . we may reimagine and recreate human institutions" (Zhao, 2020, p. 29). As we do this, we embrace protocols and expectations. We communicate clearly our needs individually and collectively. Always tuning into the relational, cognitive, and emotional that are aligned to supporting academic practices that are based on integrity, empathy, and compassion while also scaffolding and supporting the communication of research. In how we have worked both face-to-face and virtually during the pandemic we put into place feedback loops and protocols that humanise collaboration and the doing of research. This enables us to shift from disregarding the emotional wellbeing of the unseen other and to care for each other and the work (Clegg, 2009; Harley & Acord, 2011; Lee et al., 2013).

Belonging

Finding and generating a place of belonging is important. And even more so in a pandemic. In the literature, belonging is discussed in relation to the feeling of being comfortable and secure, and is profoundly rooted in attachment to a certain place (Antonsich, 2010). A sense of belonging can be viewed as a factor needed to establish and maintain positive significant relationships with others (Hagerty et al., 1992, 1996; Hall & Brault, 2021). And as such belonging has been identified as significantly impacting cognition, behaviour, and wellbeing (Allen, 2021; Allen et al., 2021; Baumeister & Leary, 1995). Belonging is fluid however, and peer support networks represent a crucial strategy for those attempting to survive and thrive in academia (Angervall & Gustafsson, 2015; Macoun & Miller, 2014).

Impacts of the COVID-19 pandemic entangled with other significant factors affecting higher education have shifted how we have worked (Oleksiyenko et al., 2020) and as scholars we have had to explore and communicate in a new context. The pandemic has disrupted traditional ways of working, and for many there has indeed been upheaval, but for us we have viewed this time as an opportunity; we see many gifts that have come our way that have disrupted inequitable, post-colonial, and physical boundaries that have been passed down to us as scholars. There has been a re-embracing of humanity with "academic communities that demonstrate the creativity, courage and freedom to challenge conventions" (Oleksiyenko et al., 2020, p. 612) in finding new ways of working that places lived experiences and connection at the heart.

Perspectives on the location of belonging

We reinterpret the halting of our collective lives, that is needing to be in a physical space with each other. We have been gifted time to stop and think and contemplate where we are and who we work with, in fact a whole reassessing of what location means. Siry (2021) suggests:

> It is of particular importance to work toward creating spaces to come together in scholarly community and to find ways to support each other. The creation of such spaces, and resultant efforts to forge relationships in new ways, can promote the creation of moral, ethical and just relationships within the wider research community.
>
> (p. 320)

For us, interrupting ways of working has demonstrated how it is possible to create and cultivate a sustainable collaboration that is borderless and has catalyzed a global belonging. From an antipodean perspective the constraints of "the tyranny of distance" with our positioning at the bottom of the world have shifted to become affordances, or at the very least equalisers, by enabling us to easily move out of our local contexts in real time. Location is repositioned to become a bonus rather than a limitation.

We have used the structures available; for instance, while many consider AERA impenetrable because of its size, the SIG structure, particularly a small SIG, provides a way to connect and belong. It has opened up our world and how we work in more sustainable ways in terms of the planet to embrace all peoples wherever they are in the world. This is particularly relevant to academic colleagues with limited means to attend face-to-face meetings, long a concern of large research organisations in wealthy countries.

We have prioritised connecting and sustaining our time together. The virtual nature of working has enhanced our collaboration. As such, virtual hanging out and a vision of how it can be different in how we can and do work together across physical borders of "countries" is embodied. We have shifted beyond the need to be physically in the same place together and to ways that embrace what it means to meaningfully collaborate. This is a paradigm shift of what is valued in the academy, the markers of success of local, national, and international that are so commonly positioned as important for progression of career trajectory (i.e. used in promotion criteria) where international publishing, attending conferences, and collaborating can only be carried out face-to-face. This is a continual othering we have interrupted. The pandemic has been a catalyst for this, a gift to disrupt unhealthy and unhelpful (traditional) ways of working and as such has provided us with a way that generates, sustains, and promotes the place of self-compassion, care, and belonging as central to who we are and how we work in higher education.

References

Allen, K. A. (2021). *The psychology of belonging*. Routledge and Taylor & Francis Group.

Allen, K. A., Kern, M. L., Rozek, C. S., McInerney, D. M., & Slavich, G. M. (2021). Belonging: A review of conceptual issues, an integrative framework, and directions for future research, *73*(1), 87–102. https://doi.org/10.1080/00049530.2021.1883409

Angervall, P., Beach, D., & Gustafsson, J. (2015). The unacknowledged value of female academic labour power for male research careers. *Higher Education Research & Development*, *34*(5), 815–827. doi:10.1080/07294360.2015.1011092

Antonsich, M. (2010). Searching for belonging – An analytical framework. *Geography Compass*, *4*(6), 644–659. https://doi.org/10.1111/J.1749-8198.2009.00317.X

Baumeister, R. F., & Leary, M. R. (1995). The need to belong: Desire for interpersonal attachments as a fundamental human motivation. *Psychological Bulletin*, *117*(3), 497–529. https://doi.org/10.1037/0033-2909.117.3.497

Clegg, S. (2009). Forms of knowing and academic development practice. *Studies in Higher Education*, *34*(4), 403–416. https://doi.org/10.1080/03075070902771937

Gay, G. (2018). *Culturally responsive teaching: Theory, research, and practice* (3rd ed.). Teachers College Press.

Hagerty, B. M. K., Lynch-Sauer, J., Patusky, K. L., Bouwsema, M., & Collier, P. (1992). Sense of belonging: A vital mental health concept. *Archives of Psychiatric Nursing*, *6*(3), 172–177.

Hagerty, B. M. K., Williams, R. A., Coyne, J. C., & Early, M. R. (1996). Sense of belonging and indicators of social and psychological functioning. *Archives of Psychiatric Nursing*, *10*(4), 235–244. https://doi.org/10.1016/S0883-9417(96)80029-X

Hall, M., & Brault, A. (2021). Academia from the Inside. In M. P. Hall & A. K. Brault (Eds.), *Academia from the Inside*. Springer International Publishing. https://doi.org/10.1007/978-3-030-83895-9

Harley, D., & Acord, S. K. (2011). *Peer review in academic promotion and publishing: Its meaning, locus and future*. Research and occasional papers Series, UC Berkeley.

Hay, J. (2019). Care is not a dirty word! Enacting an ethic of care in social work practice. *European Journal of Social Work*, *22*(3), 365–375. doi:10.1080/13691457.2017.1399253

Jarden, R., & Jarden, A. (2022). A systems pathway to self-care in academia: Me, We, and Us as avenues to integrated long-term self-care. In N. Lemon (Ed.), *Reforming our acts of self-care: Reflections on valuing wellbeing in higher education*. Routledge.

Keeling, R. P. (2014). An ethic of care in higher education: Well-being and learning. *Journal of College and Character*, *15*(3), 141–148. doi:10.1515/jcc-2014-0018

Lea, M. R., & Stierer, B. (2009). Lecturers' everyday writing as professional practice in the university as workplace: New insights into academic identities. *Studies in Higher Education*, *34*(4), 417–428. https://doi.org/10.1080/03075070902771952

Lee, C. J., Sugimoto, C. R., Zhang, G., & Cronin, B. (2013). Bias in peer review. *Journal of the American Society for Information Science and Technology*, *64*(1), 2–17. https://doi.org/10.1002/asi.22784

Lemon, N. (2021a). Vulnerability, self-care, and the relationship with us and others in higher education. In N. Lemon (Ed.), *Healthy relationships in higher education: Promoting wellbeing across academia* (pp. 1–9). Routledge. https://doi.org/10.4324/9781003144984-1

Lemon, N. (2021b). Illuminating five possible dimensions of self-care during the COVID-19 pandemic. *International Health Trends and Perspectives*, *1*(2), 161–175. https://doi.org/10.32920/ihtp.v1i2.1426

Lemon, N. (2021c). Self-care is worthy of our attention: Using our self-interest for good in higher education. In N. Lemon (Ed.), *Creating a place for self-care and wellbeing in higher education* (pp. 1–9). Routledge. https://doi.org/10.4324/9781003144397-1

Lemon, N. (Ed.). (2022). *Healthy relationships in higher education: Promoting wellbeing across academia*. Routledge.

Lemon, N. S., & McDonough, S. (2018). *Mindfulness in the academy: Practices and perspectives from scholars* (N. Lemon & S. McDonough, Eds.). Springer.

Lemon, N. S., & McDonough, S. (2021). If not now, then when? Wellbeing and whole-heartedness in education, *85*(3), 317–335. https://doi.org/10.1080/00131725.2021.1912231

Macoun, A., & Miller, D. (2014). Surviving (thriving) in academia: Feminist support networks and women ECRs. *Journal of Gender Studies, 23*(3), 287–301.

McKenzie, M., & Blenkinsop, S. (2006). An ethic of care and educational practice. *Journal of Adventure Education & Outdoor Learning, 6*(2), 91–105. https://doi.org/10.1080/14729670685200781

Mortari, L. (2016). For a pedagogy of care. *Philosophy Study, 6*(8), 455–463.

Neff, K. (2011). *Self-compassion: The proven power of being kind to yourself*. William Morrow Paperbacks.

Noddings, N. (2003). *Happiness and education*. Cambridge University Press.

Norris, J., & Sawyer, R. D. (2012). Toward a dialogic methodology. In J. Norris, R. D. Sawyer, & D. Lund (Eds.), *Duoethnography: Dialogic methods for social, health, and educational research* (pp. 9–40). Left Coast Press.

Oleksiyenko, A., Blanco, G., Hayhoe, R., Jackson, L., Lee, J., Metcalfe, A., Sivasubramaniam, M., & Zha, Q. (2020). Comparative and international higher education in a new key? Thoughts on the post-pandemic prospects of scholarship. *Compare: A Journal of Comparative and International Education, 51*(4), 612–628. https://doi.org/10.1080/03057925.2020.1838121

Roth, W-M., & Tobin, K. (2004). Cogenerative dialoguing and metaloguing: Reflexivity of processes and genres. *FQS Forum: Qualitative Social Research Sozialforschung, 5*(3), 1–12.

Siry, C. (2021). Coping and scholarship during a pandemic. *Cultural Studies of Science Education, 16*, 319–325. https://doi.org/10.1007/s11422-021-10072-6

Wolf, L. (2020). Teaching in a total institution: Toward a pedagogy of care in prison classrooms. *Journal of Prison Education and Reentry, 6*(2), 209–216.

Zhao, Y. (2020). COVID-19 as a catalyst for educational change. *Prospects, 49*, 29–33. https://doi.org/10.1007/s11125-020-09477-y

Section 2

Building compassion in our teaching during a pandemic

4 Cultivating compassion in higher education

International autoethnographic approach
to online teaching during COVID-19

Heidi Harju-Luukkainen, Jonna Kangas, David Smith,
Mhairi C Beaton, Ylva Jannok Nutti, and Rauni
Äärelä-Vihriälä

Introduction

The responses to COVID-19 have been different across the countries in the world, but nevertheless the pandemic has resulted in a state of emergency in all of them. It can be stated that COVID-19 has disrupted the "normal" routines of societies, ranging from individual lives to educational institutions and beyond. In disrupted realities, humans have a natural capacity for compassion. Compassion in human interaction can be defined as "a virtuous and intentional response to know a person, to discern their needs and ameliorate their suffering through relational understanding and action" (Sinclair et al., 2018). Further, according to Goetz et al. (2010) compassion is an action-oriented affective state and generally consists of a) an awareness of another's pain, perception of reality, and psychological state, b) a feeling of kindness, c) a yearning to mitigate the suffering, and d) doing what is within one's ability to lessen another's suffering. These definitions will be the starting point for our shared narratives and for our analyses as well. For this chapter, we have chosen an autoethnographic approach and examine personal visual and textual narratives from four different country contexts across the world. Therefore, we will be analysing our personal experiences during COVID-19. According to Ellis (2004) the autoethnographic approach seeks to describe and systematically analyse personal experiences to understand them. Just like Ludvig (2006, p. 248) describes, these narratives "do not intend to address the complexity of a full range of dimensions in a full range of categories". Therefore, our goal is to present an array of important experiences when we tried to build compassion while teaching in higher education. In more detail, *the focus in our different narratives is teaching in higher education during a global crisis and how to cultivate compassion amongst our students.* According to Ellis (2004) autoethnography is both a process and a product, which has also been the case for the development of this chapter.

The data for this study was collected from academics from four universities across the world. All universities presenting their narratives in this paper are linked through their participation in the UNITWIN/UNESCO Network

DOI: 10.4324/9781003315797-6

54 *Heidi Harju-Luukkainen et al.*

on Teacher Education for Social Justice and Diversity in Education. The UNITWIN/UNESCO program promotes international cooperation and networking between universities with the aim for participants to work collaboratively around the Sustainable Development Agenda 2030. A distinctive element of the network is that it focuses on enhancing cooperation between universities across the north/south global divide. In this research, we use international comparison as an important tool, to give readers a broader view of the subject. According to Morgan and colleagues (2010), international comparison has two goals. First, with the help of comparison we can understand any unit and, second, with the help of comparisons our understanding of different processes can become more sophisticated and complex. Further, we also suggest that we need in the look at similar processes to leverage the strength of those, as we have conducted in this chapter. From these premises this chapter is first highlighting previous research regarding compassion in higher education in teaching and learning. After that we move on towards describing the data and methods of this study. After this we present the four personal narratives and finally in the discussion part connect our results with previous research and theory.

Compassion in higher education in teaching and learning

Human beings are believed to have a natural capacity for compassion and not only towards their offspring, but more widely towards the society and others. Compassion is not an emotion, nor a logic, but it exists somewhere deeper in the human being and is understood to have multiple origins, including genetics, early childhood experiences, and social expectations and roles (Jazaieri et al., 2013). Compassion can be linked with the ethical and moral approaches of human development, for example Kohlberg and Power (1981) states that moral rules as universalisable categorical imperatives, recognisable by their formal features. In higher education the concepts of interaction, cooperation, and shared meaning-making are related with compassion and understanding of the importance of human relations. Other contemporary philosophers (like David Hume and Adam Smith) have shed light to the ethics of emotions, and the concept of "universal sympathy" as compassion. Compassion, defined by Lazarus (1991) as "being moved by another's suffering and wanting to help" (p. 289), can be considered an important feature within spiritual and philosophical development for centuries. It is also strongly related with altruism (Smith, 2009), and thus aiming to ensure that matters of caring and being related are approaches in the conceptions of morality or about real-life moral problems (Campbell & Christopher, 1996).

In educational settings, the approach to compassion can be drawn from sociocultural and cultural-historical theories of human emotions and in these theories, actions are mediated by cultural tools and activities and further with individual cultural-historical development. In this sociocultural approach compassion is not only understood as an individual trait but more as a cultural practice of an institution (Hilppö et al., 2019). In higher education institutions the scholars have not necessarily considered the role of caring and relating with students regarding their teaching work. In education the care, or intensity of relationship between a teacher and students, as explained by Dahlberg et al. (2008), is however the most common method of teaching in the academia. When coming together to focus on some shared aims, philosophies, and theories and in these moments, sharing the meaning-making process through dialogue and discussion is of importance. Further, in these moments we take and need to take into account the others' views, emotions, and positioning which can be seen as a central part of teaching in higher education. If considered from a wider perspective, Freire (1998) suggests that all education, including the academia, cannot ever be conceived without a true commitment to humanity. Freire's indispensable qualities of education focus on teachers' critical and emotional competencies to form relationships through courage, self-confidence, and respect to others. In Freire's *Pedagogy of love*, the loving relationship with students and the community could be interpreted through compassion towards humanism. In the higher education context, the compassion can be understood to build from individual teachers and the organisational culture, and it can generally consist of different components: a) an awareness of another's suffering, b) a feeling of kindness, and c) doing what is within one's ability to lessen another's suffering (Rashedi et al., 2015; Goetz et al., 2010). In general, compassion in higher educational contexts can be understood through different approaches. The first approach views compassion as developing skills and theoretical understanding of the concepts of compassion that the students take from classrooms to solve community problems, the experience in the community and their reflection on it (Rashedi et al., 2015). The second approach understands compassion as spiritual or ethical cultivation and expression of compassion. Finally, the third approach views compassion through transformative learning. Where higher education is seen as having a significant and lasting impact on a student's values, attitudes, and beliefs of care and interconnectedness. This can take place when students in higher education are not merely seen as objects of education, but participant actors who shape the values of community through social responsibility (Rashedi et al., 2015).

Visual narrative

The textual and visual data of this study, our narratives, and images come from four different countries, from four different higher-educational contexts. These are from Finland, Australia, UK, and Norway. The Norwegian context is an indigenous higher-education institution for Sámi people. Therefore, the variation of our cultural and physical contexts is wide and ranging across the north/south global divide.

In this chapter we engage with textual and visual narratives that were written and created as personal case studies. All these narratives provide a personal reflection on *teaching in higher education during a global crisis and how we individually see the cultivation of compassion amongst our students in these contexts.*

56 *Heidi Harju-Luukkainen et al.*

Our narratives show naturally cultural and other contextual differences in our higher education. These personal experiences and the differences in them are described and systematically analysed to understand them (Ellis, 2004). In each self-narrative we place the self within our social context with an overarching aim of meaning making and understanding (see also Harju-Luukkainen, 2019). However, according to McCain (2005) individual narratives reflect only a single location of each interesting dimension, which makes it difficult to account for the complexity of the whole narrative process. Further, according to Ludvig (2006, p. 248) narratives do not even intend to address the complexity of a full range of dimensions in a full range of categories. Therefore, in this chapter our aim is not to highlight the complexity, but to illustrate the similarities and divergence between our personal experiences.

Cultivating compassion in higher education across the globe

Finnish perspective – being an online future faith worker

I became an online teacher over one night when Finland was closed due COVID-19 on 17th of March 2020. The universities were immediately following the closure of society and announced that all teaching, courses, seminars, and even practicums (where our teacher students were doing their field practice training) were transformed online.

Finnish teacher education has traditionally been based on group-based classes where teachers in joint cooperation with students implement active and practical assignments which are connected to research and educational philosophy through literature and teaching. This form of practice is believed to deliver the reflective practice approach where teacher students adopt the theoretical understanding as base of their practical theory and assimilate it through critical reflection. The non-formal communication, when students refers to teachers by their first names and shares the tables in the cafeteria, supports the process of forming teacher identity and self-efficacy conceptions.

The COVID-19 closure of the university ended all this classroom and nonformal practices. Teaching was transferred online and as a teacher I soon was becoming numb staring at black screens in my online classes. When losing the opportunity to observe students' reactions and emotions teaching evoked, nor react and support those, I became unilateral and highly academic in my teaching and the playfulness and joy of exploring was diminished. The students reacted by starting to behave passive and even negative, which made me transform my teaching toward a more scientific approach and abandoning the interaction.

The next autumn on the eve of a new academic year the faculty gave a reminder to the teachers that students needed emotional support. That was kind of a wakeup call to us: compassion was vanishing behind the fear of the future and high defensive fences teachers built around themselves in a new,

Image 4.1 Visualising the empathy. Time to time I met students with my dog. Then the students dared to open their cameras with their cats and dogs around them as well.

strange situation, where all we had learned and created concerning our teaching practices was disappearing. It was time to build the trust again.

During the second COVID-19 year some practices were implemented to increase the compassion and togetherness among the staff and students. First, we started to use group works, shared essays, reflective pair approach, and other social ways of learning and doing teamwork. To make a joint essay or presentation was not only academic work for students. First time was used to learn to know other students, tell them about personal likes and dislikes in teamwork, and setting rules and goals for joint work. This was not easy through online learning platforms. The new practices also involved feedback giving and receiving skills, which were practiced through imaginative situations that would be happening during the classes. Attention was paid also on online discussion skills and communication competencies. This was done since one cannot always know for sure if the online communication involves sarcasm, comics, or for instance bad taste. It was important therefore to support students to verbalise their insecurity, conflicts of goals and performance level, and later also anxiety and loneliness during the continuing of the COVID-19 situation and university lockdown.

For teachers the new practices required time and energy, also courage to speak about personal and emotional issues with students. It required empathy to support students who suddenly burst into tears on how lonely or tired they were. It also required strong competence of communication and reflective practices: to ask students if they had listened first to others before claiming no one is hearing their voice. Compassion emerged in these situations through shared frustration, but also through support. We as teachers felt that teaching in academia was not only about transferring theoretical knowhow, but it was also about giving home and scaffolding positive faith on the future. During these moments, I was personally thinking that there is no future built by our students, if they do not dare to dream and imagine a better future.

Being an online future faith worker was not easy. It was something else I would ever dream my job in the academia would be. However, through the video call apps it was one way to make the interaction with students as natural as possible. Through interaction even more important features, such as feeling of belonging, and experiences of togetherness could be narrated.

Australian perspective – using adversity to promote positive change

The largest regional university in Australia, Charles Sturt University, has an overall student enrolment more than 43,000 students (CSU, 2021). Predominantly with campuses in New South Wales that service regional communities and international students, the University is the most experienced provider of online learning in the country and facilitates online education to domestic and international students. Like all sectors, the COVID-19 pandemic disrupted teaching, campus living, and the staff–student dynamic that forms the identity of any institution.

Australia was impacted by the pandemic later in 2020 than in Europe and for Australian universities this meant the start of the major teaching session around February/March. For Charles Sturt there were a range of impacts resulting from the various lockdowns that were implemented. There was cancellation

Image 4.2 This composite picture represents what COVID-19 meant to many academics from live presentations to working from our desk connecting via the internet.

of on-campus classes, residential schools, creative arts performances as well as social activities that are all important for campus vibrancy. There was a pragmatic realisation of the need to transfer learning to the online mode with a view to continuing student progression through their course of study. There were elements, however, that could not be transferred online, such as workplace learning or skills-based training, which created another layer of difficulty in seizing non-lockdown periods to timetable these events.

During the first teaching session, particularly at the start, there was an aura of acceptance ranging from grudging to willing. There were creative teaching solutions, impromptu communities of practice, a willingness to compromise, be patient, and in most cases, inadequacies were overlooked. However, as the forced online engagement persisted other factors combined to bring to bear psychological, physical, and economic challenges (Schneiders et al., 2022). The realities of maintaining households, maintaining businesses, caring responsibilities, and personal wellbeing affected students and staff alike, causing some students to become attrite or feel dissatisfied with their learning environment and some staff to feel isolated and have increased anxiety. The general mindset of staff and students did not consider that the temporary teaching solution would take on some permanency as the pandemic persisted and now there is much reflection on the policies, practices, and supports to enable successful learner engagement (Kift et al., 2021).

For medium to large businesses/corporations there is an ethical dilemma to the amount of support that is offered to employees in pandemic times (Robert et al., 2020). The sheer cost of supplying individual support is beyond the financial scope of these businesses yet companies do want to support their employees to make them feel valued. Charles Sturt implemented support services for staff to access for psychological and wellbeing assistance. The University also implemented special leave categories for employees that needed to isolate or care for family members to avoid annual leave being taken. There was messaging from the Vice Chancellor providing updates to university work during the pandemic and always finishing with an acknowledgement of the work that employees were accomplishing. However, there is a need to personalise this approach to reinforce the idea of community in teams and the awareness and support of colleagues in those teams. There were also impromptu virtual morning teas where colleagues would gather and share anecdotes related to managing working from home, managing issues, and managing workload. Managers saw a need to provide further support to individuals, to provide that essential personal contact (Pradies et al., 2021, p. 154). There was at least personal contact twice a teaching session, however, where required there was more contact particularly around health and welfare for individual staff members or their families. There was also contact when there were moments of innovation in teaching. The change to online teaching, online exams and individually contacting students when requests for special considerations are made were all examples used by managers to individually congratulate colleagues, acknowledging the motivation, and disseminating these exemplars across the University.

The anecdotal feedback from staff to line managers indicated an appreciation for the individual communication, acknowledging the care and recognition.

Whilst the pandemic experience caused stress in the workplace, there is also a recognition of the initiative shown by academic colleagues in their approach to teaching. The move to online teaching prompted a move to utilise more ways to engage students, to reduce moments of isolation, and to provide real time support. Part of the welfare support provided to staff is also to acknowledge the level of creativity shown by colleagues to support their students and their peers.

UK perspective – working cooperatively to meet the challenges

The lockdown occurred rapidly in the United Kingdom with little official warning. When the Prime Minister announced the national lockdown, universities were told to immediately close their campuses. Staff at Carnegie School of Education, however, had been quietly preparing for this announcement. Carnegie School of Education is part of Leeds Beckett University, a university in the north of England. As a school, we were aware of the demographic of our students; many were the first in their families to attend higher education originating from areas of high deprivation in nearby inner cities.

In normal times, the school provides a high level of pastoral care for students with a dedicated pastoral team available during office hours for face-to-face meetings – with the option of our therapy dog Betty being present – in addition to the 24-hour provision for students in crisis provided by the wider university. A key priority therefore was for pastoral care to be available immediately in a welcoming online format as we were aware that there would be high levels of anxiety due to the impact of the pandemic on the students' communities.

Image 4.3 This picture represents the ethos which our management sought to create during the pandemic that we were all "in it together" so that rather than viewing staff and students as separate entities, staff and students needed to support each other through the pandemic.

A distinctive challenge facing our students was that many of them did not own personal digital devices such as laptops. The university provides a high level of desktop computers in the library in addition to laptops which can be borrowed for up to 48 hours. With our library building closed, these were no longer available to the students who were now reliant on accessing university communications on their mobile phones. As the school accessed and distributed laptops to those students in most need, the pastoral element of provision was delivered to mobile phones and staff ensured that all teaching was delivered in a format that was readable on a mobile phone.

The staff were also aware that students were anxious about their academic progress and completion. Staff therefore began a proactive series of messages to students reassuring them of ongoing support and measures being put in place to ensure that the impact of the pandemic on their studies would be minimised including ensuring the software packages were available to permit all students to complete the academic year, the necessity for extensions to assignment deadlines to ensure no student was disadvantaged by the pandemic, and the need to seek clarification for our student teachers regarding their final school placements. The relationships and collaborative approach between staff and students that had been proactively built prior to the pandemic served invaluable as staff and students worked cooperatively to meet the challenges of the pandemic in our lives.

It is perhaps noteworthy that senior management in the school were also acutely aware of the needs of staff during this time. Aware that the staff were carrying high workloads as we adapted to the new ways of working whilst also dealing with the impact of the pandemic on our personal lives and being physically separated from each other, the senior leadership team set up a "checking in" system so that all staff received at least one video call a day to ensure their welfare. In addition to the catch-up email from our Vice-Chancellor each evening, this served to keep the staff connected with each other despite physical separation. Small tokens of appreciation were also distributed including a monthly care package containing small gifts that would contribute to individual wellbeing.

Norwegian perspective – indigenous questions in focus

Sámi University of Applied Sciences campus is in the small Sámi community Guovdageaidnu in northern Norway, and the campus gathers students and academy staff from a lot of different small Sámi communities around in Sápmi and from cities in Norway, Finland, and Sweden. The campus was the first campus in Norway to close with the aim to prevent the spread of COVID-19. At Sámi University of Applied Sciences Sámi teacher education programs are one of the main programs at Sámi University of Applied Sciences. The programs include early childhood education, primary and lower secondary school teacher education. The teacher education programs are given in Sámi language and founded on Sámi cultural practices, livelihood experiences, and cultural-based teaching

Image 4.4 This picture visualises the exchange and collaboration connected to Sámi culture we tried to recreate online in our Sámi context. In the pictures you can see students gathered outside two lávvu used by the Sámi people. Picture Mattias Sikku Valio.

views. The teaching in the programs includes gatherings on-campus approximately one week each month, teaching through practicum periods at early childhood centres and primary schools in Norway, Sweden, and Finland, and the rest of the time the teaching is online.

Initially, the online teaching continued as before, and the on-campus teaching weeks were redirected from a meeting week with face-to-face teaching at campus to an online teaching week. Rather directly, the need for implementing changes was visible as long teaching and studying days online were exhausting. The timetables needed to be reorganised, and teaching activities were spread over a longer period. Further it was needed to give space for more informal communication and collaboration between students and educational staff, and between students, and student classes. As on-campus meetings, weeks usually are a social meeting and collaboration arena where knowledge and experiences are exchanged and shared, like the traditional Sámi *servelatnja* (Sara, 2004). The traditional Sámi *searvelatnja* is a collaboration arena and meeting place where traditional works in for example reindeer herding are carried out by the reindeer herding families, and children and youth actively participate in these traditional works and thereby they become both part of a setting and learn knowledge. Taking part of traditional knowledge and being part of a social setting is important for Sámi children's and youth's experiences of well-being and it strengthens their Sámi identity (Hansen & Skaar, 2021; Nystad, 2016; Omma, 2013). Close collaboration and communication are especially important within an indigenous context, where the institution itself functions as a cultural meeting place, a meeting place where the indigenous language is used. It is important for indigenous students to be able to take part in these kinds of meeting places. This meeting place can even be one of few places where the students can use the language and exchange cultural knowledge. In Sámi teacher education, the *searvelatnja* meeting places where students and educational staff collaborate, and exchange knowledge and views, are central. Showing care and compassion for one another is central in this arena. Moving online brought new challenges to the collaboration and communication, dialogue, and to strengthen the online interaction, Sámi University of Applied Sciences started *Gáfebeavdeságastallan*-gatherings [Coffee Table conversation]. A dialogical approach can support the contextual nature of collaborative interaction, including students' perspectives and situated learning. Both students and educational staff participated during the conversations. Over a cup of coffee, educational staff informed about the planned teaching activities and tasks, students expressed their experiences and suggested changes. As the institution is a little institution with small classes, the educational staff often has a tight connection to each student and close collaboration with the students, but it was needed to make sure that students in different classes got the opportunity to meet each other and exchange experiences, and that we directly could respond to and make changes based on their experiences.

COVID-19 made the need to develop online teaching that is suitable for Sámi needs visible instead of just talking about teaching online versus at campus. Online teaching had central values as *ovttasoahpan* [collaborative learning], *iešrádalašvuohta* and *friddjavuohta* [independent and independence]. Online teaching skills are needed within the Sámi teaching professions, as many Sámi teachers teach online to pupils outside the core Sámi area. The online teaching was in the programs initially reorganised to give more students the opportunity to take Sámi teacher education, to now become online teaching that fulfil the needs of the students and the Sámi teacher profession. To address the questions of how to give online teaching, *Digigáfe* [Digital Cáfe] meetings were established as an initiative by an education staff that also became chairs for the meetings. During these meetings educational staff lifted and discussed online teaching methods and resources, and shared experiences of the use of these methods and resources. Each meeting had a special theme of focus, the chair could for example present an online teaching resource, let everyone try it out, and afterwards we discussed the possible use of it in Sámi teacher education. This development is needed as the Sámi teacher education programs demand a high level of distance learning and the students need to both take part in interactive teaching in different settings and with different types of contents and knowledge and learn methods of how to teach online to be able to interact with future pupils.

Discussion

The responses to COVID-19 have been different across the countries in the world, and it resulted in different actions in the higher education contexts in all of them. However, according to Goetz et al. (2010) compassion is an action-oriented affective state and generally consists of a) an awareness of another's pain, perception of reality, and psychological state, b) a feeling of kindness c) a yearning to mitigate the suffering and d) doing what is within one's ability to lessen another's suffering. In this study our aim was to present the gist of important experiences when we tried building compassion in higher education contexts. In more detail, the focus in our different narratives is teaching in higher education during a global crisis and how to cultivate compassion amongst our students. According to the results our narratives tell of individual and context appropriate solutions developed by each institution and the narratives revealed a need to develop solutions also for future sustainability. In our narratives, COVID-19 made us rethink the educational framework on three levels in the academic contexts: 1) administrational level, 2) operational level, and 3) individual level. On all these levels the response in building compassion amongst our students happened differently. This had most likely to do with our different social as well as physical contexts of our higher education institutions.

In the Norwegian Sámi context, challenges to collaboration, interaction, dialogue, and communication in a cultural context with the students were met with culturally adapted *Gáfebeavdeságastallan*-gatherings [Coffee Table conversation] led by the teachers. In these situations, students were able to connect to the Sámi culture and traditions and feel belonging as well as share meanings. In the Australian context, in similar challenges, the staff began a proactive series of messages to students to highlight compassion and empathy; in the UK as well, the staff ensured that all teaching was delivered in a format that was readable on a mobile phone. In Finland focus was also paid to online discussion skills both for students as well as for staff. In Finland for teachers the new practices required time and energy, also courage to speak about personal and emotional issues with students. In all these different examples the higher education staff related with their students during as well as outside the classes and the reactions to the need were met on different levels in the academic system. This is not possible without compassion towards one another, which then creates togetherness and a sense of security for the students as well as for the staff in higher education.

Compassion is seen as an action-oriented affective state (Goetz et al., 2010) and therefore, we would like to take this notion further to a practical level from the basis of our narratives and analysis. We suggest that in a time of crisis, students can be supported in multiple ways on three different levels in the academic context (administrational, operational, and individual) by

1) Active communication that underlines compassion and empathy
2) Active interaction that supports feeling of belonging and experiences of togetherness
3) Ensuring teaching and communication that resonates with the cultural context
4) Highlighting equity in access to information

According to Rashedi et al. (2015) higher education is seen as having a significant and lasting impact on a students' values, attitudes, and beliefs of care and interconnectedness. This can take place when students in higher education are not merely seen as objects of education, but participant actors who shape the values of community through social responsibility. This is an important takeaway, visible in all our narratives. In the Finnish context the teacher expressed herself as being a future faith worker, caring for students' wellbeing in multiple ways during teaching. In the Sámi context the student's community building was at the core of the teaching and through this student's wellbeing. The teacher's wellbeing was not forgotten either. In the UK a "checking in" system was put into place that all staff received at least one video call a day to ensure their welfare. Also in Australia, staff got access for psychological and wellbeing assistance, when needed. As a summary, the students needed to be cared about and valued, as well as the faculty. In these processes both student and personnel can be and should be supported towards compassion, in a time of a global crisis.

References

Campbell, R. L., & Christopher, J. C. (1996). Moral development theory: A critique of its Kantian presuppositions. *Developmental Review, 16*(1), 1–47.

CSU. (2021). *Charles Sturt at a glance 2020*. Retrieved February 23, 2022, from https://cdn. csu.edu.au/__data/assets/pdf_file/0007/3810787/2020-CSU-At-A-Glance.pdf

Ellis, C. (2004). *The ethnographic I: A methodological novel about autoethnography*. AltaMira Press.

Freire, P. (1998). *Teachers as cultural workers: Letters to those who dare to teach*. Boul Westview.

Goetz, J. L., Keltner, D., & Simon-Thomas, E. (2010). Compassion: An evolutionary analysis and empirical review. *Psychological Bulletin, 136*, 351–374.

Harju-Luukkainen, H. (2019). "We would love to have you over . . .": Building career capital in a new academic environment. In A. Black & S. Garvis (Eds.), *Women activating agency in academia: Metaphors, manifestos and memoir*. Routledge. https://doi. org/10.4324/9781315147451

Hilppö, J. A., Rajala, A., & Lipponen, L. (2019). Compassion in children's peer cultures. In G. Barton & S. Garvis (Eds.), *Compassion and empathy in educational contexts* (pp. 79–95). Palgrave Macmillan. https://doi.org/10.1007/978-3-030-18925-9_5

Jazaieri, H., Jinpa, T. G., McGonigal, K. M., Rosenberg, E., Finkelstein, J., Simon-Thomas, E., . . . Goldin, P. R. (2013). Enhancing compassion: A randomized controlled trial of a compassion cultivation training program. *Journal of Happiness Studies, 14*, 1113–1126.

Kift, S., Thomas, L., & Shah, M. (2021). Retention and success in the midst of a pandemic. In *Student retention and success in higher education* (pp. 295–333). Palgrave Macmillan.

Kohlberg, L., & Power, C. (1981). Moral development, religious thinking, & the question of a seventh stage. In L. Kohlberg (Eds.), *Essays on moral development, vol. 1: The philosophy of moral development* (pp. 311–372). Harper & Row.

Ludvig, A. (2006). Differences between women? Intersecting voices in a female narrative. *European Journal of Women's Studies, 13*(3), 245–258.

Pradies, C., Aust, I., Bednarek, R., Brandl, J., Carmine, S., Cheal, J., Pina e Cunha, M., Gaim, M., Keegan, A., Lê, J. K., & Miron-Spektor, E. (2021). The lived experience of paradox: How individuals navigate tensions during the pandemic crisis. *Journal of Management Inquiry, 30*(2), 154–167.

66 *Heidi Harju-Luukkainen et al.*

Rashedi, R., Plante, T. G., & Callister, E. S. (2015). Compassion development in higher education. *Journal of Psychology and Theology, 43*(2), 131–139.

Robert, R., Kentish-Barnes, N., Boyer, A., Laurent, A., Azoulay, E., & Reignier, J. (2020). Ethical dilemmas due to the COVID-19 pandemic. *Annals of Intensive Care, 10*(1), 1–9.

Schneiders, M. L., Mackworth-Young, C. R., & Cheah, P. Y. (2022). Between division and connection: A qualitative study of the impact of COVID-19 restrictions on social relationships in the United Kingdom. *Welcome Open Research, 7*(6), 6.

Sinclair, S., Hack, T. F., Raffin-Bouchal, S., McClement, S., Stajduhar, K., Singh, P., . . . Chochinov, H. M. (2018). What are healthcare providers' understandings and experiences of compassion? The healthcare compassion model: A grounded theory study of healthcare providers in Canada. *BMJ Open, 8*(3), e019701.

Smith, T. W. (2009). Loving and caring in the United States: Trends and correlates of empathy, altruism, and related constructs. In B. Fehr, S. Sprecher, & L. G. Underwood's (Eds.), *The science of compassionate love: Theory, research, and applications* (pp. 81–120). Wiley-Blackwell.

Taggart, G. (2016). Compassionate pedagogy: The ethics of care in early childhood professionalism. *European Early Childhood Education Research Journal, 24*(2), 173–185. https://doi.org/10.1080/1350293X.2014.970847

5 "It's gonna be alright"

Self-compassion for us and students during COVID-19

Gwen Erlam and Kay Hammond

Introduction

The COVID-19 pandemic has left people feeling anxious and grieving for the loss of loved ones and freedoms once taken for granted. The unpredictable chaotic nature of this crisis affected everyone not only in their physical health, but in their mental wellbeing. Societal inequalities are exposed (Henrickson, 2020), and 'normal realities' are shifted in ways not previously imaginable. The pandemic and related social lockdowns have accelerated the need for online and remote teaching within university settings. Due to the abrupt nature of the pandemic, many students and educators were not prepared for this forced transition, resulting in increased anxiety among both educators and students.

This chapter outlines how we, two course educators, navigated the initial 'storm' of the pandemic regarding managing student anxiety and stress while at the same time managing our own stressors. We communicated with students through weekly announcements which often contained visual elements designed to encourage a sense of compassion, hope, and wellbeing. In this way, we aimed to quell the 'fires' emerging in the early part of the pandemic by showing compassion and a pathway whereby students (and ourselves) could begin to manage our stress. This chapter reviews how we employed these communications during the developing storm of the pandemic to engender a sense of, "It will be alright."

Context

Showing compassion

According to the Oxford University Press (n.d.) *compassion* comes from the ecclesiastical Latin stem *compati*, or to "suffer with." Suffering in one form or another has been part of everyone's experience over the COVID-19 pandemic. During this pandemic turmoil, students often found their studies a distraction, not a focus. Educators found themselves suffering with their students as together we experienced aspects of the social trauma brought on by the pandemic, while at the same time trying to move forward to reach our potential in higher education.

DOI: 10.4324/9781003315797-7

68 Gwen Erlam and Kay Hammond

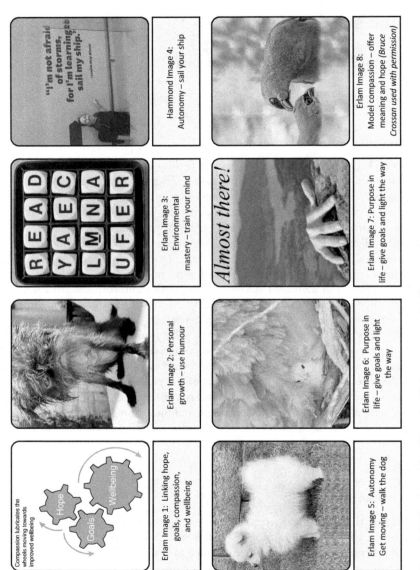

Image 5.1 Visual narrative illustrating focus, strategy, and self-care routines.

Compassion has been recognised as central to national processes of reconciliation and forgiveness after societal trauma (Erskine, 2020). Compassion is an important foundation for teamwork, management, leadership, intimate relationships, and democratic citizenship (D'Amico Guthrie et al., 2014). The experience of the pandemic necessitated the need for compassion to move us through this crisis towards a sense of reconciliation within ourselves and with each other. One author (Martinez, 2020, p. 2) noted, "The genuine presence of another person during crisis moments is one of the most potent drugs of humanity." Individuals can find hope and meaning if they feel they are not alone – that someone else cares to know their situation. Educators need to model compassion throughout the educational process The best way to teach compassion is to live and speak its language (Martinez, 2020). Furthermore, research shows there is a direct, positive relationship between compassion and hope (D'Amico Guthrie et al., 2014). Show compassion and students will have a more hopeful outlook. Without compassion, hope and meaning can slip away.

In this chapter we examine our reflective journals and extracts from our online course, noting ways we extended compassion to our students. Using Ryff and Singer's (2008) model of psychological wellbeing, we analyse how each of the six dimensions (i.e., *Positive relationships, Personal growth, Self-acceptance, Environmental mastery, Autonomy, and Purpose in life*) influence wellbeing.

Wellbeing is profoundly shaped by the surrounding contexts of people's lives. During the pandemic, *hope* often fueled the pursuit of goals (e.g., survival, place to work, food, financial resources, etc.). *Compassion* provided often-needed incentive motivating individuals to achieve their goals. The result was an enhanced sense of *wellbeing*. In essence, compassion, hope, and wellbeing are inextricably linked and work together synergistically to assist in goal achievement.

We present extracts from our online course and reflective journals to illustrate our strategies of showing compassion in our course communications as we guided students and ourselves to reach our potential. Through our announcements (including images and compassionate words), we directed students to take small steps which would assist them in achieving the learning outcomes for the course. The course content and assessments provided a path forward, but students required compassion to take the necessary risks. It is good to keep in mind that wellbeing is profoundly influenced by the surrounding contexts of people's lives, and as such, the opportunities for self-realisation are not equally distributed (Ryff & Singer, 2008).

Methodological approach

Appreciative inquiry as a research approach was loosely employed to collect this data. This asset-based methodology to organisational and social engagement uses questions to uncover the strengths, advantages, and/or opportunities occurring in communities, organisations, or teams (Godwin & Stavros,

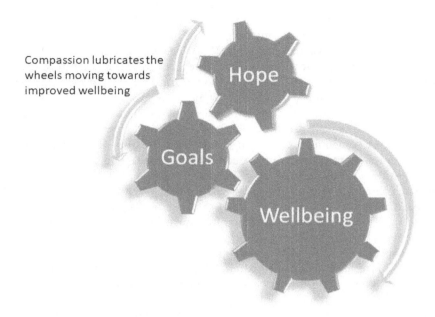

Image 5.2 Linking hope, goals, compassion, and wellbeing (Erlam).

2021; Townsin, 2021). We found this approach kept us positive and looking for the beneficial and life-giving aspects of life during the pandemic. Appreciative inquiry impacts how we interact with others and with ourselves so that we can be with our families, clients, and organisations in the best possible manner.

Literature (positioning of strategy/self-care focus)

Self-care strategies for maximising wellbeing and compassion

During the pandemic we were challenged with managing our personal lives while juggling the university context and all that it involves. Stress became a constant companion requiring that we either dust off or integrate self-care strategies into our lives. Self-care has a dual purpose of fostering our wellbeing as educators, while at the same time helping us encourage these same skills in students (Warren & Deckert, 2020). Wellbeing involves the continual process of developing one's potential and is influenced by many factors (Hughes & Burke, 2018). The concept of self-actualisation, as formulated by Maslow, is centrally concerned with the realisation of personal potential (Ryff & Singer, 2008). However, we are never in a process of completion regarding wellbeing. We are continually developing and becoming rather than achieving a fixed state. So, to help students develop, we considered several aspects of wellbeing using Ryff and Singer's (2008) six dimensions of wellbeing designed to move people toward maximising their personal potential.

- **Positive relationships**: This dimension involves the ability to develop warm, satisfying, and trusting relationships. Concern for the welfare of others, strong empathy, affection, and intimacy are key along with an understanding of the give and take of human relationships.
- **Personal growth**: Of all the aspects of wellbeing, this dimension comes the closest in meaning to Aristotle's *eudaimonia*. It is concerned with self-realisation of the individual involving a continual process of developing one's potential.
- **Self-acceptance**: This dimension involves the ability to know ourselves, and in doing so to accurately perceive our own actions, motivations, and feelings. Ultimately, it is the need to have positive self-regard – a central feature of mental health.
- **Environmental mastery**: This dimension involves an individual's ability to choose or create environments suitable to favourable psychic conditions. This key characteristic of mental health involves the ability to extend the self and participate in significant spheres of endeavour that go beyond the self (Allport, 1961).
- **Autonomy**: This dimension emphasises qualities such as self-determination, independence, and the regulation of behaviour from within (Maslow, 1968). Individuals with autonomy resist enculturation. A fully autonomous person has an internal locus of evaluation and does not look to others for approval, instead evaluating oneself by personal standards (Rogers, 1962).
- **Purpose in life**: This dimension involves helping people find meaning in their travails and suffering. This dimension involves having a clear comprehension of life's purpose along with a sense of direction and intentionality.

(Ryff & Singer, 2008, p. 29)

The following section maps these dimensions of wellbeing onto the communication strategies we used in our online course during the pandemic. In the context of the pandemic, we found ourselves needing to deal with basic survival first – this involved our immediate relationships with the students and each other. We therefore begin with Ryff and Singer's (2008) dimension of *Positive Relationships* and move into the other dimensions in no particular order.

Strategies (tips)

Positive relationships – *we're still here*

When the first lockdown occurred, the initial response was to step back and reassess our pedagogical approach (i.e., how to put all content online). An unfortunate result of this was a disconnection between staff and students as courses were put "on hold." We realised that our first step needed to be to let our students know that *"we're still here!"* Subsequent communications focused on building relationships to reduce student anxiety as we developed a way forward. The following announcement was our first communication after the lockdown occurred.

> We are hoping you are all safe and well in your bubbles. We are still here (though isolated) but wanted to reassure you that we are working to ensure that when we resume classes, you will have a positive experience.
>
> (Course announcement 27 March 2020)

The goal of this announcement was to initiate a social bond by acknowledging that like the students, we were also isolated and feeling the same 'pain.' Using the words 'reassure' and 'positive experience,' we were inviting an ongoing positive relationship between us and the hundreds of students we were communicating with.

Research has shown that educator behaviours and strategies appear to inform students' motivation to engage with learning (Wood, 2017). There are some things that we do, either intentionally or by accident, that appear to have a positive effect on the motivational processes being formed by students. One effective strategy is to build positive relationships with students from the initial phases of the course. These positive relationships have the potential to encourage engagement, which has come to be regarded as essential in assuring students' enthusiasm for learning while improving the quality of their relationships with educators and other students (Wood, 2017).

There are four different types of engagement which have been identified. These are affective engagement, cognitive engagement, behavioural engagement, and agentic engagement (Wood, 2017). Affective engagement encompasses the positive and negative reactions to educators, fellow students, and schools. This type of engagement is presumed to create ties to an institution and influence willingness to do the work involved in completing a course (Fredricks, 2011). Indicators of positive affective engagement include enthusiasm, interest, enjoyment, satisfaction, pride, vitality, and zest (Wood, 2017). These indicators came back to us in the form of communications from students after tutorials or announcements. We felt excited that student feedback (usually in groups after online tutorials) showed our communications were effective. One student stated:

> Everything makes sense, is logically expressed and all the assignments are in order with sufficient time. I really enjoy this course.
>
> (Personal communication 30 May 2020)

This student showed affective engagement and was motivated by the clear presentation accompanied with communication (both verbally and in writing) to meet course goals. This clarity motivated them to do their best.

Cognitive engagement is an internalised process so can only be observed from self-reported perceptions (Wood, 2017). One student reported, "The material online was helpful, extensive, and very useful." This student showed active cognitive engagement with the course content. Cognitive engagement acts as the mediating bridge between context and learning outcomes. Therefore, the pass rates for a course are an indicator that student effort has been exerted to comprehend complex ideas and master skills. This course (semester 1, 2020) had 612 students with a 98% pass rate. This was encouraging to us as a teaching team as it demonstrated evidence of good cognitive engagement.

Behavioural engagement refers to those participating in and completing learning activities. In this course 98% passed with 2% either withdrawing or not completing. To keep students progressing through the course, we made a concerted effort to communicate 'next tasks' and how to best manage these in the allotted time. One student emailed us stating, "I was always kept up to date on what was going on and what was expected of me." This comment helped us know that our communication was encouraging good behavioural engagement.

Agentic engagement refers to the extent to which a student feels efficacious in self-determining and being successful within active learning contexts (Wood, 2017). This type of engagement centres on volitional cognitive contributions that students make to learning activities presented by the educator. In other words, do students willingly engage with the content and exert energy to learn. We knew we were achieving in agentic engagement when we got feedback that, "The online tutorials really helped me focus on what to concentrate on for the assessments." This feedback inspired us to continue developing positive relationships through our communication. Another strategy we began to explore was the use of humour, which ties into Ryff and Singer's (2008) dimension of *Personal Growth*.

Personal growth – *look at the bright side!*

Research has shown that there is a positive link between what is deemed 'light humour' and mindfulness. Humour is an umbrella term for everything funny and laughable (Roeckelein, 2002). It allows us to observe, recognise, accept, and let the present moment pass without judging it (Hofmann et al., 2020). When carefully implemented, humour may be fruitfully combined in a positive personal intervention, as well as in the professional teaching space, to enhance wellbeing. In fact, humour and mindfulness can mutually influence each other leading to personal growth in the area of wellbeing (Hofmann et al., 2020). The resultant synergy between the two helps in fostering a benevolent view of the world which assists individuals in managing stressful circumstances. Shared humour is a powerful way for people to bond and talk about the stressful circumstances they may be experiencing. Humour can reduce hostility and the resultant production of endorphins can strengthen the immune system (Kreger, 2008). Additionally, mindfulness (paying attention to the present moment and

Image 5.3 Personal growth – use humour (Erlam).

being non-judgmental) is enhanced by these light forms of humour (Hofmann et al., 2020).

A playful frame of mind is one condition essential for humour. To foster this, we showed humorous images to convey a sense of compassion and 'we get it' in response to student stress. We used the following exert in an announcement:

> While we realise that all of us are feeling a bit 'frazzled,' as the photo indicates. You can console yourself with the fact that we are almost through with this semester. Press into the pain and you will find that your hard work will be rewarded. You can do this!
>
> (Announcement 27 September 2020)

This ability to accept and 'let go' during the ups and downs of stressful circumstances is an aspect of mindfulness which allows us to take difficult seasons more lightly. The use of humour also extends beyond positive relationships and can create aspects of personal growth. Being able to look at a situation from a more objective and less negative manner (through humour) can also enhance Ryff and Singer's (2008) dimensions of *Personal Growth* and *Self-acceptance*, thus improving overall wellbeing.

Self-acceptance – *you're ok!*

Self-acceptance is described as the ability to be in contact with one's internal, private experience and be able to assimilate and accommodate this experience into self-knowledge in a positive and accepting manner (Bruno et al., 2020). This positive self-regard is associated with mental health and higher levels of life satisfaction. Self-acceptance is an adaptive psychological concept which plays an important part in regulation of psychological needs. It is important in promoting psychological flexibility, smoothing self-criticism, and accepting painful private experience (Bruno et al., 2020). It is important that educators foster self-acceptance even amid perceived student failure (i.e., not turning in assignments, extension requests, etc.), to encourage psychological flexibility. An example of this was in a course announcement prior to the first written assessment:

> We loved seeing so many of you at the online tutorials last week. Your engagement with us in the course content was marvelous to see! We were glad that even those of you who were just lurking got so much benefit from being there too. Remember to apply for special consideration if you have experienced anything that may have affected your ability to complete your assessment – that's what it's there for.
>
> (Course announcement 9 August 2021)

This announcement encouraged students to accept themselves in whatever level of participation they were able to offer during tutorials. It also encouraged them to normalise any disruptive life events and apply for an extension without shame. We noted that we had about half of the students requesting extensions in this unprecedented time. This suggests that we successfully normalised this process.

Environmental mastery (training the mind) – *engage in the "climb"*

Encouraging contemplative practice can be achieved by encouraging students to focus attention, deepen understanding of course content, develop compassion for those around them, and explore their mind's capacities (Warren & Deckert, 2020). As a team we encouraged students during tutorials and online discussion boards to think deeply and increase the complexity of their thinking (Ryff and Singer's (2008) *Environmental Mastery*). The following announcement

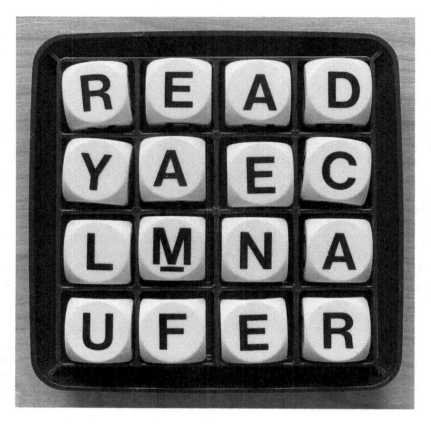

Image 5.4 Environmental mastery – train your mind (Erlam).

is an example of our encouragement to dig deeper into the course content with an accompanying visual image:

> You will not be able to skim read this article and get the answers. You will have to 'critically engage with this article to find these nuances.' This will require a steeper climb than the first article, but I am confident that you all can do it! This is like looking for difficult-to-find words in boggle – go for the detail!
>
> (Course announcement 27 April 2021)

The above post encourages students to dig deeper into the content, but with a whimsical image that can reduce stress and motivate at the same time. The image is a reminder to connect, or indeed reconnect with what is most meaningful. In the turbulent times of the pandemic, reminding students of previous happier times (i.e., playing games with significant others) can encourage self-care. This development of a critical first-person perspective can encourage both students and educators to examine their own experience in relationship to the content they are studying, thus transforming their understanding of how their learning can affect their actions in the world (Warren & Deckert, 2020).

Autonomy – *in study, learn to sail your own ship*!

At the outset of the pandemic, both educators and students felt stressed about how the course would proceed and what our day-to-day life would look like. This response was due to the distraction of media reports, case numbers, deaths, and vaccination rates. Both students and educators lost a sense of control over personal and academic pursuits leaving us in a state of turmoil.

Autonomy in the form of *being able to regulate one's behaviour internally* during a crisis is important for both students and educators. It is important to realise one's ability to manage a situation without looking for the approval of others. Autonomy in this sense contributes to overall wellbeing.

The course shifted from a blended format to fully online during the pandemic. This meant that students had to have some agency (direction) to study on their own without external incentives. It became necessary to motivate them with positive goal-setting announcements and then rely on their independence and self-determination to get the job done. One example of this was a student announcement which encouraged students to think of how to navigate their study journey:

> It is great to see many of you have attempted the first test at least once. Use your first attempt as feedback and revise to boost your learning and test score for the second attempt. You have one more week until the first test closes. It can feel a bit rough when you are learning new concepts but keep at it and your sailing will become smoother! Be a courageous learner!
> Kia Kaha and keep sailing!
>
> (Course announcement 23 July 2021)

Below is one student's assessment of this online strategy:

> I enjoyed the learning sessions being readily available online. This meant I could learn and progress in my <u>own time</u>. It was great that [the lecturers] continued to communicate well even through COVID-19.
>
> (Student communication semester 1, 2020)

This student was giving evidence of their own self-regulation. They were able to work independently relying on an internal locus of motivation despite the extraordinary circumstances of the pandemic. These qualities embody Ryff and Singer's (2008) dimension of *Autonomy*.

Mindfulness as a practice can help to increase autonomy. It is defined as the ability to focus and maintain attention to both internal and external experiences

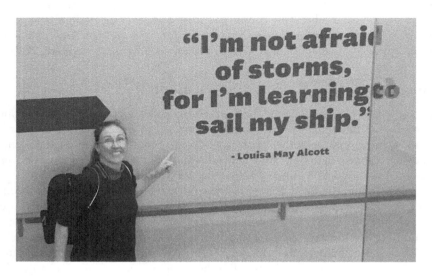

Image 5.5 Autonomy – sail your ship (Hammond).

while employing an accepting and non-judgmental attitude (Bruno et al., 2020). It encompasses a loosely grouped set of methods that serve to encourage reflection and contemplative practice (Warren & Deckert, 2020).

In our course, we encouraged students to be autonomous by posting lectures in an asynchronous manner. The lectures were in an MP4 format and were interlaced with relevant video clips to enhance interest and engagement. They could watch these lectures at any time and in any place and thus create their own learning space. We gave them an overall timeline and due dates for each assessment and then encouraged them, in the form of announcements and emails, to work at their own pace. The discussion board was used as a contemplative space where they could post questions and view what other students were thinking. In this way we invited them to self-regulate and become autonomous. They were encouraged to show agency and choice to regulate their behaviour.

We urged students to spend time outside in nature and take things a day at a time. Examples of these strategies included daily walks and focusing on small joys in life (e.g., a good conversation, a bike ride, a cup of coffee). Through email and announcements, we promoted spending time in solitude and silence (Warren & Deckert, 2020), away from the chaos of the pandemic. We endeavoured to show compassion for each other and students. Below is an announcement with the accompanying image prompting self-care and compassion while encouraging autonomy:

> Please take care of yourselves and your families. I went on a walk today with my puppy and saw a fantail. She said she didn't know a thing about COVID-19 – what bliss!
>
> (Course Announcement 17 April 2020)

Image 5.6 Autonomy, get moving – walk the dog (Erlam).

This announcement prompts readers to make daily choices to take care of their physical health. Autonomy emphasises qualities such as self-determination, independence, and the regulation of behaviour from within (Maslow, 1968). Individuals with autonomy make choices using an internal locus of evaluation (e.g., make decision to walk daily, do assignment, etc.) without looking for approval from others. One student's response to the earlier announcement was as follows:

> Your little messages of assurance at the end of each announcement demonstrate how caring you are of someone's mental health. If no one has messaged you to tell you how your simple words have brightened their day (especially someone like me a stressed-out university student), well, let me [be] the first to tell you how much I appreciate it during this time.
> (Personal communication 31 May 2020)

It was encouraging to us as educators to know that our communication was being heard and influencing student mindfulness and overall wellbeing.

Purpose in life – give goals and light the way

When the pandemic began, both students and educators found themselves grasping for a shred of hope amidst the chaos – whether it was a vaccine or another job to help pay the bills. It is important to realise that hope itself is not taught, nor is it awakened by imparting cognitive skills or coping strategies. Hope Theory assumes that human behaviour is goal directed and that goals provide the targets for hopeful thinking (Snyder, 2002). There is a powerful connection between compassion, which helps provide the goal, and hope which helps us to achieve the goal (D'Amico Guthrie et al., 2014).

Snyder (2002) defines hope as "the perceived capability to derive pathways to desired goals and motivate oneself via agency thinking to use those pathways" (p. 249). The key component here involves developing *means* to achieve goals. This is termed *agency* and involves the ability to carry out tasks to achieve goals.

Educator actions that engender hope are often perceived as compassionate and enabling on the part of students. Hope allows individuals to gain renewed *Purpose in Life* and meaning in the midst of suffering coupled with a clear sense of direction and intentionality (Ryff & Singer, 2008). As educators it is important to attempt to encourage both components (goals and agency) thus fostering a sense of hope for students. Hope is ignited when receiving compassion (D'Amico Guthrie et al., 2014) in the form of encouraging motivation (agency) while highlighting a path towards a goal. The effect is like a flashlight shining on a desired path. The flashlight shows the way (agency) to the goal. The following announcement shows both goals and agency and was designed to inspire hope for our students. The image inspires hope in the form of new beginnings.

> This announcement comes with our best wishes that all is going well for you and your families in your level 4 bubbles. Well done on making it through this unprecedented time. Tomorrow begins a new season in this adventure (Level 3 lockdown). For this upcoming week please check that you are attending to the following:
>
> - Make sure you have attempted all sections of Tests 1&2 (close May 7th);
> - Work carefully on Assessment 1 (due May 4th 4PM); and
> - Check the announcement section of this course for tutorial times.
>
> Know that we are supporting you and looking forward to reconnecting online. Best wishes as the semester enters this new season.
>
> (Course Announcement 28 January 2022)

Educator actions that have been identified as compassionate and as engendering hope are encouragement, problem solving, responsive empathy, and affirming that good choices can bring about good futures (D'Amico Guthrie et al., 2014). Students build their hope by internalising their educators' compassion. With this in mind, we endeavoured to provide clear goals in our course followed by an achievable pathway to reach these goals (peppered with 'you can do it' comments). We relied on research that shows that when students overcome obstacles, their level of hope increases and they can become more flexible

Image 5.7 Purpose in life – give goals and light the way (Erlam).

and creative in reaching their goals (D'Amico Guthrie et al., 2014). Another example was an announcement posted during the pandemic (below) gave both a pathway and agency to students:

> I know many of you are struggling to get to the top of this mountain of work, but you are ALMOST THERE! Do not give up on yourselves or your ability to finish this! You can do it! Assessment 2 is due tomorrow at 4PM. The recorded tutorial is up under the tutorial tab if you couldn't attend one.
>
> Remember that it does not have to be perfect. Many of you have had a very hard time this semester so give yourself a bit of grace – you've got this! Very Warmest Regards in what has been a terribly challenging year.
> (Course Announcement 4 October 2020)

Image 5.8 Purpose in life – give goals and light the way (Erlam).

This announcement shows that we as a teaching team have been learning better ways to engender hope through compassion extended to our students during this unprecedented time. The above announcement tied into several aspects of Ryff and Singer's (2008) dimensions including *Positive relationships, Personal growth, Self-acceptance, Environmental mastery, Autonomy, and Purpose in life*. By encouraging students to believe in themselves while gently guiding them towards a path to achieve their goals, their sense of hope and wellbeing can grow. Hope is ignited by receiving compassion. Confidence to tackle future situations can be a lasting effect.

Discussion

Compassion fundamentally contributes to the wellbeing of individuals and society (Rynes et al., 2012). Compassion is essential to a strategy aimed at improved wellness. Additionally, a compassionate attitude towards others' suffering activates the reward pathways in the brain contributing to gratifying feelings (Kim et al., 2009). Taking a compassionate attitude towards another enables a deeper understanding of the suffering being experienced.

All of this provides rationale for why we included strong elements of compassion in our communications to reach students online during the pandemic.

The emotion of compassion includes three cognitive beliefs: that the other person's suffering is serious (not trivial), that it is unmerited, and that it is something that might befall any of us (Gallagher, 2009). If it is true that compassion does contribute to wellbeing, it is useful to view compassion through the lens of Ryff and Singer's (2008) six dimensions of wellbeing: *Positive relationships, Personal growth, Self-acceptance, Environmental mastery, Autonomy, and Purpose in life*. We found our focus on positive relationships led naturally to supporting the other dimensions of wellbeing. Together they work to move us toward maximising our personal potential. As educators our role involves incorporating these dimensions into our teaching in a manner which enables students to develop towards more positive wellbeing. These efforts, when applied effectively, promote human flourishing by training the mind (Dahl & Davidson, 2019).

Ryff and Singer's (2008) dimensions of wellbeing provide a meaningful framework to support initiatives in demonstrating compassion and providing hope for our students. We used a variety of different communications and activities to maximise self-care in an environment dearth of strategies essential to studying during a pandemic. We noted students responded positively to the images of animals that accompanied many announcements. We recommend that educators build a collection of images they can associate with dimensions of wellbeing to encourage students in their online courses. For example, in the future we plan to use the following image to illustrate compassion.

Image 5.9 Model compassion – offer meaning and hope (Erlam). (Photo: Bruce Crossan, used with permission).

Gwen Erlam and Kay Hammond

We provided connection and compassion during a time when we needed it ourselves. As educators, embedding some of these strategies into our courses and personal lives helps us to become living examples of the outcomes we wanted to achieve. The best way to teach compassion is to live and speak its language (Martinez, 2020). At the end of this pandemic, we will not only be remembered by our competence, but by our compassion.

Conclusion

The pandemic provided a springboard for launching into new directions regarding how we communicated to students and worked together as a team. Caring communication between ourselves and our students was essential amidst the uncertainties of the pandemic. We developed ways to show compassion to our students thus inspiring hope and an improved sense of wellbeing as defined by Ryff and Singer (2008). These strategies included: developing positive relationships; encouraging personal growth through contemplative practices (including self-acceptance); inspiring students to train their minds and move towards environmental mastery; stirring students to work independently relying on an internal locus of motivation; and employing humour to lighten the 'darkness' and improve wellbeing. Additionally, we used compassion with its two-pronged dimensions of agency and pathway to inspire hope for the future. We communicated compassion, kindness, and a general message of, "It will be alright."

References

Allport, G. W. (1961). *Pattern and growth in personality*. Holt, Reinhart & Winston.

Bruno, F., António Branco, V., Ana Nunes, S., & Telma, M. (2020). Relationships between emotional schemas, mindfulness, self-compassion and unconditional self-acceptance on the regulation of psychological needs. *Research in Psychotherapy, 23*(2). https://doi.org/10.4081/ripppo.2020.442

Dahl, C. J., & Davidson, R. J. (2019). Mindfulness and the contemplative life: Pathways to connection, insight, and purpose. *Current Opinion in Psychology, 28*, 60–64. https://doi.org/10.1016/j.copsyc.2018.11.007

D'Amico Guthrie, D., Smith Ellison, V., Sami, K., & Tyson McCrea, K. (2014). Clients' hope arises from social workers' compassion: African American youths' perspectives on surmounting the obstacles of disadvantage. *Families in Society: Journal of Contemporary Social Services, 95*(2), 131–139. https://doi.org/10.1606/1044-3894.2014.95.17

Erskine, R. G. (2020). Compassion, hope, and forgiveness in the therapeutic dialogue. *International Journal of Integrative Psychotherapy, 11*, 1–13. www.integrative-journal.com/index.php/ijip/article/view/159/102

Fredricks, J. A. (2011). Engagement in school and out-of-school contexts: A multidimensional view of engagement. *Theory into Practice, 50*(4), 327–335. https://doi.org/10.1080/00405841.2011.607401

Gallagher, P. (2009). The grounding of forgiveness: Martha Nussbaum on compassion and mercy. *The American Journal of Economics and Sociology, 68*(1), 231–252. https://doi.org/10.1111/j.1536-7150.2008.00622.x

Godwin, L. N., & Stavros, J. (2021). Appreciative inquiry: A life-giving personal operating system. *AI Practitioner, 23*(1). https://doi.org/10.12781/978-1-907549-46-5-10

Henrickson, M. (2020). Kiwis and COVID-19: The Aotearoa New Zealand response to the global pandemic. *The International Journal of Community and Social Development, 2*(2), 121–133. https://doi.org/10.1177/2516602620932558

Hofmann, J., Heintz, S., Pang, D., & Ruch, W. (2020). Differential relationships of light and darker forms of humor with mindfulness. *Applied Research in Quality of Life, 15*(2), 369–393. https://doi.org/10.1007/s11482-018-9698-9

Hughes, N., & Burke, J. (2018). Sleeping with the frenemy: How restricting 'bedroom use' of smartphones impacts happiness and wellbeing. *Computers in Human Behavior, 85*, 236–244. https://doi.org/10.1016/j.chb.2018.03.047

Kim, J.-W., Kim, S.-E., Kim, J.-J., Jeong, B., Park, C.-H., Son, A. R., Song, J. E., & Ki, S. W. (2009). Compassionate attitude towards others' suffering activates the mesolimbic neural system. *Neuropsychologia, 47*(10), 2073–2081. https://doi.org/10.1016/j.neuropsychologia.2009.03.017

Kreger, R. (2008). *The essential family guide to borderline personality disorder: New tools and techniques to stop walking on eggshells.* Hazelden.

Martinez, R. C. K. (2020). Compassion as caring in crisis: Reflections of an educator. *Journal of Health and Caring Sciences, 2*(1). https://doi.org/10.37719/jhcs.2020.v2i1.e001

Maslow, A. H. (1968). *Toward a psychology of being* (2nd ed.). Van Nostrand.

Oxford University Press (n.d.). Compassion. In *Oxford English Dictionary.* Retrieved October 21, 2021, from, http://www.oed.com/viewdictionaryentry/Entry/11125

Roeckelein, J. E. (2002). *The psychology of humor: A reference guide and annotated bibliography.* Greenwood Press/Greenwood Publishing Group.

Rogers, C. R. (1962). The interpersonal relationship: The core of guidance. *Harvard Educational Review, 32*(4), 416–429.

Ryff, C. D., & Singer, B. H. (2008). Know thyself and become what you are: A eudaimonic approach to psychological well-being. *Journal of Happiness Studies, 9*, 13–39. https://doi.org/10.1007/s10902-006-9019-0

Rynes, S. L., Bartunek, J. M., Dutton, J. E., & Margolis, J. D. (2012). Care and compassion through an organizational lens: Opening up new possibilities. *Academy of Management Review, 37*(4), 503–523. https://doi.org/10.5465/ami.2012.0124

Snyder, C. R. (2002). Hope theory: Rainbows in the mind. *Psychological Inquiry, 13*(4), 249–275. https://doi.org/10.1207/s15327965pli1304_01

Townsin, J. (2021). *Introduction to appreciative inquiry.* Champlain College. https://appreciativeinquiry.champlain.edu/learn/appreciative-inquiry-introduction/

Warren, S., & Deckert, J. C. (2020). Contemplative practices for self-care in the social work classroom. *Social Work, 65*(1), 11–20. https://doi.org/10.1093/sw/swz039

Wood, R. (2017). *The influence of teacher-student relationships and feedback on students' engagement with learning.* Cambridge Scholars Publishing.

6   Cultivating a language of compassion in higher education

Maarika Piispanen and Merja Meriläinen

Introduction and study background

The changes are said to occur slowly because the intrinsic reaction of people to change in the supposed normal is an instinct for protection. That is, in a changing situation, one seeks to preserve oneself and find safety. We are reminded of this in the work of Kurt Lewin and the Change Management Model, which proposes that whenever driving forces are stronger than restraining forces, the status quo or equilibrium will change.

COVID-19 was an uninvited, unknown guest. The changes it brought with it were visible everywhere. As teachers at the university, we found ourselves in a very sensitive situation: we had to guide and teach a large group of adult students who lived in uncertainty, maybe even in fear. Many students felt alone, as too did their families and loved ones, with so much change. One of the changes that occurred for students was distance learning. Learning was brought into the home, and with this a general uncertainty, including uncertainty about the progression of their own studies, and eventually the study itself.

As teacher educators we had to react quickly to changes. Although the situation was new to us too, we wanted to offer our students compassionate and safe learning experiences thorough the course, just as we had been doing earlier, before the pandemic. We shared our thoughts by writing and talking about them to each other. As we reflected and processed our own and collective response to the pandemic and shifting to distance learning, we decided to design the course to best support students. We needed to make sure we took into consideration studying remotely from homes, where the family would be present, and that the effects of COVID-19 would be present but in ways we couldn't at this stage still know how. The more we reflected we realised we needed to capture this moment in time. As researchers, we were aware that the data we collected from mostly spontaneous discussions, both written and spoken, would become valuable to us later. From our reflections we were noticing that the earlier, formal guidelines and course structure were put aside and more compassionate and supportive tools took place in these discussions (Lapadat, 2017a, 2017b; Pink, 2009).

DOI: 10.4324/9781003315797-8

Cultivating a language of compassion in higher education 87

The students we were supporting were final year preservice teachers. As a part of their study and professional development they spend time in educational settings; this is often called practicum or professional experience. During the final practicum students begun to work as substitute primary school teachers in grades one to six in Finnish comprehensive schools, all around Finland. The complexities of teacher preparation were highlighted even more so during the pandemic. Working alone with no peer support, no face-to-face supervising or counselling, busy evenings with families, maybe even distance teaching from homes, where student´s own children were studying in distance as well, challenged us all. At this time, we understood that we had to create a new kind of guidance system to support and meet students' needs, fears, and challenges at the right time in right ways during the practicum. Also, the professional needs like classroom management skills, common and specific pedagogical issues, or questions of pupil's special needs were present and needed to be supported in many ways.

The visual narrative described above crystallises the key points of entry in our study and reflections: compassionate encounter, ubiquitous learning (multi-location), peer learning, the development of reflective thinking skills, and a sense of community. These key points tell in their own way the compassion that guided the course design and served as the investigative glue and the central background idea of discussions for us with our students. Our conscious

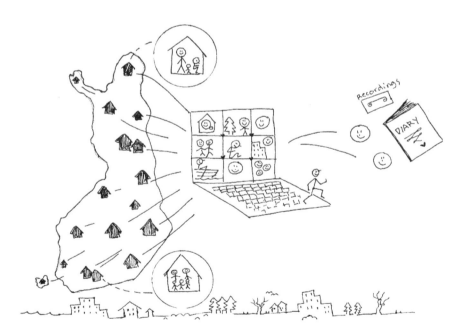

Image 6.1 Shows the realisation of the study in the form of a short visual narrative.

88 Maarika Piispanen and Merja Meriläinen

thinking led to the idea to make the final practicum possible for all participants so that every student and us, teachers as well, could participate in the process from the middle of everyone's own lives, from the life situations that each person would live at that moment. The goal was to merge studies into life rather than assimilate life into a part of studies. For us as teachers and researchers, the brightening and acceptance of this kind of thinking also required time and new creative thinking to see what good, flexible, timely consideration of the life situation of the student can bring to each person and how we manage to see them as possibilities.

Research method

In this framework, where the data was collected from our own thoughts, discussions, feelings, and emotions, an autoethnographic research method was a natural choice for us. Combining our personal experiences (auto), which by analysing (graph) we seek to create an understanding of cultural experience (ethnos) (Ellis et al., 2010). Autoethnographic research is a form of qualitative data, the method seeks to describe and methodically study personal experience to understand cultural experience. It is characterised by narrative: telling is a writing strategy that, in this study, made visible the meanings that emerged through discourse analysis and created intelligibility and scientific credibility in them (Pink, 2009; Winkler, 2018). This narrative could be seen as an expedition and a voyage of discovery, of which we were together with the students.

The key concepts and elements of this autoethnographic research associated with running the compassionate teaching practice emerged. Revealed was the importance of ubiquitous learning environments with a spirit of community. In this community we valued individual lived experiences, timely ways to show abilities and growth during the course, strengthening the good, and individual and group supervision underpinned by compassionate interaction in all kinds of encountering with self and each other.

The diverse material we draw upon in this autoethnographic research consists mainly of written texts and recordings in relation to its social context, COVID-19, which naturally led us to choose discourse analysis as a methodological choice. According to Pietikäinen and Mäntynen (2009, pp. 52–53) discourse analysis is a research method for studying written or spoken language in relation to its social context. It aims to understand how language is used in real life situations – just like language, the discourses will give us tools to describe the world and its events, build our identity in it and offer us resources that give it all meaning. With our research material, we wanted to look at what kind of discourses emerged from our discussions, and how they evolved during the process. In the spring of 2020, we, as teachers, were also in front of the new and experienced a certain kind of similarity with students in changing situations, such as remote work, for example. In the first discussions, there are more reflections on the structures and pedagogical arrangements of teaching,

Cultivating a language of compassion in higher education   89

Table 6.1 Describes the Number of Students Enrolled in Each Course as well as the Averages of the Course Grades.

	The name of the course			
	Pre-school and elementary pedagogy (May-June 2020)	*Finnish language and literature 6 ECTS credits (May–June 2020)*	*A1 Early language Learning 3 ECTS credits (May 2021)*	*Teaching practicum 8 ECTS credits (August-September 2021)*
Number of participants	24	39	22	24
Average grade scale 1—5	4.6	5	4.4	5
Passed the course %	100	97	100	100

while when the studies began, our discussions focused more on the themes of compassionate confrontation with students.

Trust carries believing in your students

The measures of success in studies at the university include the credits and completion of courses. Competence is demonstrated by grades, which in this case were presented on a scale of one to five. The compassionate angle of entry and compassionate planning for the courses, presented in this chapter, concerned primary school teacher students who started their studies at Kokkola University Consortium Chydenius in January 2020. This research intervention looked at four different courses of study, two of which took place between May and June 2020, one in May 2021 and one in August/September 2021 (see Table 6.1).

Discourses related to the figures, described in Table 6.1, most featured comments relating to interaction and feedback written to students. Discourses highlight reflections on compassionate and student resource enhancing speech and used language, which we associate as relevant factors in student success. Student feedback, on the other hand, highlights carefully prepared feedback, the versatility of feedback and the beautiful and kind words present in them, pedagogically meaningful and skillfully crafted courses, and a sense of community, which came to prominence, particularly in cases, where social support was included during study as part of the learning process.

Compassionate interaction as a resilience builder

When COVID-19 arrived, we were just getting ready for teaching. The fast pace of the pandemic took off quickly. We had to transform both in our minds and planning to move to remote delivery. Around us, societal discourse focused on challenges, which for its part increased anxiety in the teacher educator environment, but also among the students. Right from the start it was obvious for us that we would focus on opportunities, changing and challenging perspectives that focused on challenges that were commonly raised in discussions. Supported by positive and solution-focused perspectives, we set out to plan and implement the final practicum in learning environments and ways that would promote students' wellbeing.

Compassion and self-compassion, empathy, encounter presence, and reinforcement of a sense of community and resilience formed the course design of the red thread. These were planned to appear in all course tasks, ways of working, feedback, and the many opportunities of learning in the environments our students were working in. We began to write a course manuscript from these points of views, keeping in our minds that teachers are the engine that drives social and emotional practices in schools and classrooms, and their own social-emotional competence and wellbeing strongly influence their students.

We brought beauty with positive quotes and nice pictures related to quotes to the e-learning platform, Moodle, that were used to share the course material. The introduction pages to all five course modules included tasks that were planned to empower students' resilience and the use of their personal character strengths. Everyone completed a personal Values in action strengths assessment (also known as VIA) (Peterson & Seligman, 2004) as part of the guidance process to support identifying top strengths that can be engaged with and support ways of engaging with self and others. Students also completed a resilience tree worksheet to make visible things that will empower their resilience during this time and in life commonly. Students read articles and viewed webinars that scaffolded their thinking and understanding to solution-focused ways of approaching their professional development at this time. We focused more on positive perspectives and gave them tools to create healthy learning environments that they could transfer to their own pupils as well.

We both, as teacher educators, who are also qualified work supervisors as well as therapists, found the process of renewing our curriculum to be more compassionate focused quite natural. And by the end, we found the integration of the framework encompassed curriculum, the community we formed, and the whole practicum guidance process.

We set ourselves two questions as teacher educators that we perceived to be relevant in designing the final learning process. The first question was targeted to the learning process itself: is it possible to design a process so that learning would be a cohesive experience for everyone to some extent? The other question was targeted to both common and individual needs in that process: on the other hand, could we design processes so that it would be an empowering experience common to everyone, where, however, we would seek to consider also other individual needs than those, emerging from the individuality of learning? With joint discussions and deliberations, we concluded that this is possible. We ended up designing a weekly educative-pedagogical work supervision small group process, with eight to ten students in each group. The process was planned for the first six weeks to support and empower students to achieve the course goals in time.

In the educative way of working, the equality and open dialogue between us as teacher educators and the students were emphasised. Educability is commonly associated with the idea of giving, teaching, or learning knowledge, due to the origin of the word, education, which is translated as: education, teaching, civilisation, or educational doctrine. According to the definition of Kemm and Close (1995), an educative approach is a planned, systematic process used to influence the behaviour of another. This requires changes in knowledge, attitudes, and skills (Kemm & Close, 1995). Participation in dialogue offers both instructor and supervisors new opportunities to develop and learn in their own rhythm. That is something we found extremely important in supervision discusses with our students. Scaffolding and learning in one´s personal zone of proximal development allowed the students to trust themselves as professionals. In successful educative supervision group meetings, we could see how the shared interaction process reinforced the ability to produce more diverse and shared knowledge. Thus supporting and providing opportunity for all group members to open up a willingness to share their ideas, understanding, experiences, and findings of the professional growth during the practicum (Ylönen, 2019).

Social interaction, resilience, and change are strongly linked to each other, these emerged in the discussions we had in relation to future courses. Social interaction in online learning can lead to increased student engagement, motivation, and can help improve student performance. This was something we already had found earlier, before COVID-19. As teacher educators, we discussed on several occasions how we could create opportunities for meaningful and sustained social interactions during the online courses, especially when multiple online courses were going on at the same time. We acknowledged that as humans we have a strong need to connect and relate with other individuals by developing cooperation and perspective-taking. The ability to make social connections, group living, and sharing resources had a selective advantage in coping with physical and psychological stress. Social connections and support are also causal components of resilience.

The concept of resilience is described in the research literature as an individual's ability to tolerate adversity and as a skill to return to a more functional state after adversity (Waugh, 2014). Resilience is also connected to the mental capacity of the individual, which allows one to, often unconsciously, exploit the resources and strengths that sustain one's wellbeing in various situations (Koirikivi & Benjamin, 2020). As teachers, we considered which comes first, social interaction or resilience. The change in students' everyday life brought about by COVID-19 took place just at the stage of the start of their teacher studies. We discussed whether we had managed to support resilience both as individuals and collectively. We considered: are we strong enough now for change, or were we in a situation where our students' resilience was still vulnerable in relation to learning? How do we manage to transform difficulties into resources and initiate a process in which support for the other also begins to form a process for strengthening its own resilience, as part of the learning processes for studies? To these questions, we did not find one correct answer. The strength of our own resilience cannot be measured other than in adversity and on the other hand, we could not know what kind of adversity we would face as the spring progressed. We couldn't fight against COVID-19, so we decided to influence how we experience it, and how we reflect our feelings on others (Ojanen, 2021).

In recent decades, resilience has been studied not only by the individual aspect but also as a common skill of the group, and especially as a characteristic that emerges in social interaction. We, as teachers and researchers, also wanted to pay special attention to it in this study, where the factors of interaction and resilience, compassion and self-compassion rise from our material into a key to many locks. Zautra (2014, pp. 185–193) states "the interaction serves as the baseline growth base for resilience". Especially in situations where individuals support each other with sympathy, connections suggestive of resilience growth have been observed (Poulin et al., 2013; Zautra, 2014). Revealed further is the dynamic nature of resilience, "by developing its own interaction skills and weighing the personal attitudes and patterns of action in relation to other people and communities, reflecting, mirroring and, with it, reinforcing our own resilience competency" (Zautra, 2014, p. 189). Psychologist Ojanen (2021) aptly states, "when the changes are surprising, sudden, and negative, they cause frustration and stress, which is further exacerbated by the rush". These unconscious states of mind and emotion erupt into interactions, leaving the capacity of the community to be compromised. According to resilience researchers (e.g. Zautra, 2014), however, there is also a possibility here that the interaction or situation may provoke empathy and a sense of being "in the same boat", thus supporting the other reinforces the resilience of both the one supported and the supporter.

A reciprocal chain reaction can be possible. This is exactly what Zautra (2014) offered us as teachers and researchers to work with – this can also be seen in discussions emerging from the research material. These discourses relate in several situations to our observations that we have made about student feedback, for example:

> I am grateful that you have taken the time to read our thoughts. Your feedback was supportive and gave a sense that you are really interested in what we have learned and reflected on during the courses.
>
> The feedback you gave me also strengthened my understanding about my own learning. This was a very pleasant thing to note for me personally.
>
> Even if we never met face-to-face during the course, then, at least for me, there was a feeling that I have been across.

Such feedback reinforced our views that the depth of interaction and encounter cannot be measured by distance length. It is about a genuine interest and encounter, which comes from an atmosphere of compassion. It is a desire to confront and bring the student an awareness that we are fellow travellers.

The importance of planning a compassionate learning process

The importance of planning a compassionate learning process emerged as a key discourse to us: we came to understand that we should enable a diverse, ubiquitous learning environment that would provide students with the opportunity to study both alone and together and would allow knowledge to be demonstrated in many ways in the right time to each one. This approach allowed us to convey the feeling that it is possible for our students to achieve the goals set for their studies precisely at the level of competence that they felt is possible in this new life situation. With our own compassionate attitude, we would support and strengthen each student's self-compassionate attitude towards themselves, thereby promoting resilience growth in everyone (Zautra, 2014). Experiencing compassion works somewhat two-way. First, to have compassion for others you must notice that they are suffering, that everyone is suffering. This is the common humanity aspect of compassion. Second, compassion involves feeling moved by others' suffering so that your heart responds to their pain. When this occurs, you feel warmth, caring, and the desire to help the suffering person in some way. Having compassion also means that you offer understanding and kindness to others when they fail or make mistakes, rather than judging them harshly. Finally, when you feel compassion for another, it means that you realise that suffering, failure, and imperfection is part of the shared human experience (Brown & Okun, 2014). From this point of view, we also saw the fact that learning processes should enable sharing shared and lived experiences to support others, such as in joint small group meetings as part of learning processes. Even if we were each in our shelters, we could increase the feelings of support and community in an otherwise uncertain situation by adding different forms of compassion and attention to the different stages of the learning process.

It is revealed in our discourses that it was significant to us to understand the concept of resilience, allowing the individual through their own activities to communally strengthen the protective factors needed in the resilience process, such as social responsibility, adaptability, resilience, goal-oriented, interactivity and good self-esteem (Richardson, 2002). How compassionately we would approach students in interactions related to learning situations, would affect how we also strengthen their resilience to cope with challenging situations. Bradley et al. (2014, pp. 199–200) states that such communally reinforced resilience requires the successful adoption of cognitive, emotional, and behavioral norms, which contribute to laying the groundwork for self-regulation, emotional regulatory skills and psychic for the development of psychological flexibility and social competence. Mental flexibility refers to, for example, an individual's ability to convert to different perspectives, while strong social competence manifests itself, among other things, as psychosocial skills that will grow and maintain constructive interpersonal relationships. As teacher educators and researchers, we think that both mental flexibility and psychosocial skills played a central role in building a successful learning process. The new

94 *Maarika Piispanen and Merja Meriläinen*

ways of studying remotely, time and place unbound, and the ability to interact in social interaction, flex, and message, rose to prominent positions from both individual welfare and community welfare perspectives.

Compassionate approach as a pedagogical strategy

> If you want others to be happy, practice compassion. If you want to be happy, practice compassion. – Dalai Lama

Gilbert (2014) aptly defines compassion as "sensitivity to suffering in oneself and others". As we processed the pandemic and the changes it brought us, we wanted to respect and consider the diverse life situations of students. We did this by focusing on opportunities with ways of studying at home. Our discussions focused on compassionate and encouraging encountering with students, not just course demands. We soon realised that a compassionate approach seemed to be a pedagogical strategy that embraced individual and collective stress in a way that promoted security, resilience, and self-efficacy. By being compassionate in our delivery and with pedagogical decisions we helped students believe in themselves, to cope the course, and feel empowered.

In our view, the redesign of courses and related learning processes was the only correct decision we could make. Our actions allowed us to reinforce compassion and student resilience. By this, we mean that in a situation of change, we wanted to create something totally new, both pedagogically and emotionally, to support students to achieve their learning goals. In this process, we used our earlier discussions about taking account of compassionate interaction to promote self-compassion, in order to support student welfare and coping during their studies. We chose methods that allowed them to study without binding students to a specific time, place, or manner. This allowed students to feel empowered as individuals with the opportunity to commit to the course in the best possible ways (Biggs, 2003; Meriläinen & Piispanen, 2016). When designing the learning experience, we considered it important that students have the choice of how to make their skills visible: in what form, alone or in combination with others. By acknowledging our students come with different life situations, opportunities and abilities to study in learning environments, we designed our courses as flexible as possible.

According to Richardson's (2002) metatheory of mental resilience, when an individual faces a sudden change, as we perceive distance learning caused by COVID-19, a person's survival is put to a hard test. The theory provides a simple model of resilience as a process occurring in different life situations, where the individual's own situational activity rises to be relevant, by which he can influence the outcome of possible survival. In a situation like that, one can act either consciously or unconsciously, thus attaching emotions and thoughts in one direction out of three: a) loss, which we describe as jamming in the study. We associate this with the sudden end of teaching at the campus; b) return to baseline homeostasis, which involves moving past the disruption, described in research by the desire to continue as earlier. In considering the pandemic and study on campus, this direction was not possible. As the best option for wellbeing, Richardson (2002) presents c) resilient reintegration, where adaptation leads to a higher level of homeostasis. This is where we position our integration of compassion into courses during the COVID-19 pandemic. Richardson (2002) also presents an alternative where an individual's ability to act becomes crippled in the face of an entirely new situation. This is described as a dysfunctional state, where maladaptive strategies (e.g., self-destructive behaviors) are used to cope with the stressor. COVID-19 ruled out both the first and second option put forward by Richardson in this theory in our opinion. We understood that the only correct way for us a teacher educators was to approach planning a course by resilient reintegration. The fourth alternative, a dysfunctional state, could have led to suspension of teacher studies, which was unreasonably not an option to us.

We understood quite early during the planning of courses the that if we did not design the courses to be flexible and thus enable a wide range of ways to study and provide temporal looseness to complete studies, progress in studies could be among some students quite challenging. We were also aware of the potential of our activities to support resilience from the perspectives of strengthening good and compassionate speech. At best an individual can handle the change that has occurred at both thought and emotional levels so that it gives new insights and strengths to life, and thus creates an even stronger mental resilience and skill to cope with challenging life situations (Richardson, 2002, pp. 311–312). By affirming good, we mean embodying compassionate, empathetic, and empowering encounters. We did this in the ways that we consciously reinforced in our conversations with students both face-to-face and in using various other channels of communication. In our discussions, we tried systematically to strengthen students in accordance with solution-focused theory, allowing students to notice and draw attention to those things that were working or were well at that moment (de Jong & Berg, 1997). This reinforcement of good and attention to the good things of the moment strengthened positive thinking, goal setting, and orientation towards themselves, others, and situations being experienced. In this way, we directed the student to orient action and think away from the things they perceived to be challenging for themself. We also supported them in search of solutions for things they felt like challenging. The most challenging situations in students' speech from the students' point of view were the organisation of study time during family everyday life. This included both the challenge of finding time for a small group to work together and the challenge of participating in some teachings at precisely a certain time of day. These messages reinforced our own planning process. Studies independent of time and place, timely guidance, learning processes that promote learning and compassionate and prescient guidance were important matters.

In the same context, we consider the importance of compassionate speech as part of student wellbeing and its support and promotion. In the discourses, we linked compassion to walking alongside the student and empathising with their situation. Finally, as described earlier in this chapter, we ended up providing students with opportunities for educative-pedagogical work supervision, which would help them structure their own thinking and thus promote their own coping. Incorporating work supervision into future courses is reflected in discourses as discussion content related to student encounters and the importance of compassionate speech in strengthening resilience. We felt this was connected first and foremost with the strengthening of students' learner image and sense of self-ability. To support this, we established students social support meetings at both the individual and group level. In such community discussions, emotional and interactional skills, as well as peer support, are emerging as relevant factors supporting resilience and coping (Richardson, 2002). To represent this, Image 6.2 shows the compassionate and supportive learning process and the key discourses emerging from the dialogue between two university teachers relating to the compassionate study course planning process promoting student wellbeing and learning. This we call our COVID-19 Framework in the years 2020–2021.

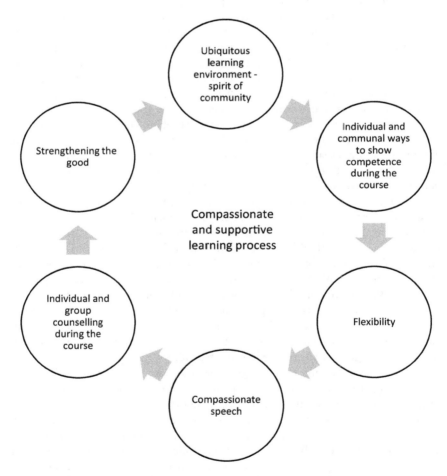

Image 6.2 The compassionate and supportive learning process during COVID-19.

Conclusion

Abraham Maslow (1943, p. 380) has stated that people's primary psychological need is to be allowed to experience affection and love with others. The fundamental need for affection and love, together with identification with emotions, create for us an emotional state that leads to the action called compassion. From its root words, it means feel with someone. Compassion refers to both an understanding of another's pain and the desire to somehow mitigate that pain.

In this autoethnographic study, we experienced the meanings of compassion on many levels. At first, we could not imagine the multidimensional network of compassion that our reflection, the discourses emerging from them and the theoretical examination of them, as well as living in processes, would take us as researchers. The compassion we as researchers experienced for students delivered us a gift, cultivating our own resilience to cope with the challenges that change brought. At the same time, it highlighted the good around and gave rise to a compassionate learning community that supported one another in learning progress and professional growth.

Compassion is outlined to consist of three elements that reflect a different functional process. At the first level, a person can consider the emotional states (knowledge) of another person. The observation of the suffering of another person is the most critical level of experiencing compassion, as it requires a certain degree of openness to the environment, which is not always possible due to environmental factors. On the second level, a person reaches for a desire to help the other (feeling). And on the third level, the feeling is refined into acts of helping (acts) (Kanov et al., 2004). During the intervention, a worldwide pandemic affected us all, which is why challenges and adversity were easy to notice. Space was born into a sense of conscience – we were not stuck in adversity, but we moved through this feeling and turned the challenge into an opportunity to create something new and meaningful (Richardson, 2002). As we moved through the process, the social nature of a sense of compassion appears, where compassion originates from another person's emotion. We were able to imagine others' experiencing pain and, through that, obtain the necessary information about the situation of another (Kanov et al., 2004, p. 812). In our notes, we can read how the empathy we experienced for students and our own transition to work from home helped us as teachers and researchers empathise with the situation of students with compassion. As physical presence changed and we connected only through the web, we felt the importance of enabling the culture of compassionate and empathetic encounter to be realised and to find practices that work with it to achieve a common sense of community and cohesion (Ruutu & Salmimies, 2015, p. 79).

A solution-focused empowering approach played a critical role in not getting caught in the negative, but rather deliberately working to strengthen those resources and the good that we experienced and found in the situation. The changes to university study brought by COVID-19 led us as teacher educators to consider the challenges that the changes brought to the everyday life and lives of

98   *Maarika Piispanen and Merja Meriläinen*

the students. This, in turn, created an innate desire to help and support each other and students in the best possible ways that were possible in the rapid time frame of change. This was critical to supporting and promoting student wellbeing. We call this chain of events the information base provided by empathy, which led to the start of the third level of compassion that Kanov et al. (2004) present.

Our exploration with a compassionate approach emerged as a key factor in the discovery of new forms of community. Amid this discovery, many also found themselves in a new way. Articulating our journey has allowed us to illustrate new perspectives on our personal experience, on epiphanies, as Goodall (2001) calls them, by finding and filling the gap in existing, related storylines, which there are yet many, in the field of compassion and compassionate approach to teaching in higher education.

References

Biggs, J. (2003). *Teaching for quality learning at university – what the student does?* (2nd ed.). SRHE/Open University Press.

Bovey, W. H., & Hede, A. (2001). Resistance to organisational change: The role of defence mechanisms. *Journal of Managerial Psychology, 16*(7), 534–548.

Bradley, B., Davis, T. A., Kaye, J., & Wingo, A. (2014). Developmental social factors as promoters of resilience in childhood and adolescence. In M. Kent, M. C. Davis, & J. W. Reich (Eds.), *The resilience handbook: Approaches to stress and trauma* (pp. 197–208). Routledge/Taylor & Francis Group.

Brown, S. L., & Okun, M. A. (2014). Using the caregiver system model to explain the resilience-related benefits older adults derive from volunteering. In M. Kent, M. C. Davis, & J. W. Reich (Eds.), *The resilience handbook: Approaches to stress and trauma* (pp. 169–182). Routledge/Taylor & Francis Group.

Dalai Lama, & Cutler, H. C. (2002). *Onnellisuuden taito.* Elämän opaskirja. Tammi.

de Jong, P., & Berg, I. K. (1997). *Interviewing for solutions.* Brooks/Cole.

Ellis, C., Adams, T. E., & Bochner, A. P. (2010). Autoethnography: An overview. Forum qualitative Sozialforschung/forum: *Qualitative Social Research, 12*(1). www.qualitative-research.net/index.php/fqs/article/view/1589/3095

Gilbert, P. (2014). The origins and nature of compassion focused therapy. *British Journal of Clinical Psychology, 53*(1), 6–41.

Goodall, B. H. L. (2001). *Writing the new ethnography.* AltaMira.

Kanov, J. M., Maitlis, S., Worline, M. C., Dutton, J. E., Frost, P. J., & Lilius, J. M. (2004). Compassion in organizational life. *American Behavioral Scientist, 47*(6), 808–827.

Kemm, J., & Close, A. (1995). *Health promotion: Theory and practice.* MacMillan.

Koirikivi, P., & Benjamin, S. (2020). Mitä resilienssi on? *Koulutus, kasvatus ja oppiminen.* https://www2.helsinki.fi/fi/uutiset/koulutus-kasvatus-ja-oppiminen/mita-resilienssi-on

Lapadat, J. C. (2017a). *Health promotion: Theory and practice.* Macmillan.

Lapadat, J. C. (2017b). Ethics in autoethnography and collaborative autoethnography. *Qualitative Inquiry, 23*(8), 589–603.

Maslow, A. H. (1943). A theory of human motivation. *Psychological Review, 50*(4), 370–396.

Meriläinen, M., & Piispanen, M. (2016). From everyman's right to everyman's possibility. In C. A. Shoniregun, & G. A. Akmayeva (Eds.), *Ireland international conference on education. Proceedings of IICE* (pp. 200–206). Infonomics Society.

Ojanen, V. (2021). *Jaksaakseen työelämän jatkuvassa muutoksessa, on tunnettava itsensä paremmin.* Telma. https://telma-lehti.fi/psykologi-ville-ojanen-jaksaakseen-tyoelaman-jatkuvassa-muutoksessa-on-tunnettava-itsensa-paremmin.

Peterson, C., & Seligman, M. E. P. (2004). *Character strengths and virtues: A handbook and classification.* American Psychological Association; Oxford University Press.

Piderit, S. K. (2000). Rethinking resistance and recognizing ambivalence: A 110 multi-dimensional view of attitudes toward an organizational change. *Academy of Management Review, 25*(4), 783–794.

Pietikäinen, S., & Mäntynen, A. (2009). *Kurssi kohti diskurssia.* Vastapaino.

Pink, S. (2009). *Doing sensory ethnography.* Sage.

Poulin, M. J., Brown, S. L., Dillard, A. J., & Smith, D. M. (2013). Giving to others and the association between stress and mortality. *American Journal of Public Health, 103*(9), 1649–1655.

Richardson, G. E. (2002). The metatheory of resilience and resiliency. *Journal of Clinical Psychology, 58,* 307–321.

Ruutu, S., & Salmimies, R. (2015). *Työnohjaajan opas. Valmentava ja ratkaisukeskeinen ote.* Pro Talentum.

Waugh, C. E. (2014). The regulatory power of positive emotions in stress: A temporal-functional approach. In M. Kent, M. C. Davis, & J. W. Reich (Eds.), *The resilience handbook: Approaches to stress and trauma* (pp. 73–85). Routledge/Taylor & Francis Group.

Winkler, I. (2018). Doing autoethnography: Facing challenges, taking choices, accepting responsibilities. *Qualitative Inquiry, 24*(4), 236–247.

Ylönen, K. (2019). *Dialoginen ohjaus ammatillisen kehittymisen tukena. Työpaikkaohjaajan opas.* Grano.

Zautra, A. J. (2014). Resilience is social, after all. In M. Kent, M. C. Davis, & J. W. Reich (Eds.), *The resilience handbook: Approaches to stress and trauma* (pp. 185–196). Routledge/Taylor & Francis Group.

Section 3

The personal and professional blur

Work–life family balance
with COVID-19

7 The personal and professional blur

Work-life family balance with COVID-19

Tina Yngvesson, Ann-Charlott Wank, and Susanne Garvis

Introduction

On the 17th November 2019 the first case of COVID-19 was detected in the Wuhan province of China (WHO, 2022b). At the time of writing the pandemic has been ongoing for two years and according to the World Health Organization (2022b) 349,641,119 cases of COVID-19 have been reported, including 5,592,266 deaths. Across the globe, health services have been under chronic strain and most areas of people's lives worldwide have been disrupted (Unadkat & Farquhar, 2020). Common for most sectors globally is that the more pressured the situation becomes, the more important it is to pay attention to one's own wellbeing. The paradox, however, is that in some sectors, such as education, there are other social actors, students and pupils, whose demands and rights oftentimes are catered to first. It is commonly accepted that the pandemic is not a sprint, rather it is a marathon that requires many sectors across the globe to adjust, adapt, and deliver the best possible teaching and learning for the duration of the marathon (Unadkat & Farquhar, 2020). In order to do this, we must first look after ourselves and our colleagues, so as not to collapse entirely. In other words, supporting oneself through providing oneself with care "has never been more important; we must give ourselves permission to change" (Unadkat & Farquhar, 2020). One way to provide this care is to engage in what is commonly known as "self-care". The World Health Organization defines self-care as "the ability of individuals, families and communities to promote health, prevent disease, maintain health, and to cope with illness and disability with or without the support of a healthcare provider" (WHO, 2022a). Thus, self-care can be understood as the process of taking care of oneself through engaging in behaviours and activities that promote personal health and also an active management of symptoms of illness if and when these occur. This management can be executed through making conscious and well-informed choices in regard to nutrition (dietary choices), lifestyle (e.g., quality and length of sleep, movement and exercise, time spent away from work and/or chores resting), environmental factors (e.g., social habits, extracurricular commitments, living conditions) and socioeconomic factors (e.g., cultural beliefs,

DOI: 10.4324/9781003315797-10

community support, income level) and also self-medication (dietary supplements, non-prescription drugs, so-called "comfort food",[1] alcohol intake). Hence, the scope of self-care as understood by the WHO includes,

> health promotion; disease prevention and control; self-medication; providing care to dependent persons; seeking hospital/specialist care if necessary; and rehabilitation including palliative care. Inherent in the concept is the recognition that whatever factors and processes may determine behaviour, and whether or not self-care is effective and interfaces appropriately with professional care, it is the individual person who acts (or does not act) to preserve health or respond to symptoms.
>
> (WHO, 2022a)

Executing self-care with the overarching aim of achieving wellbeing can be assumed against the background from a few core principles. These are self-reliance, empowerment, autonomy, personal responsibility, self-efficacy, and greater community (e.g., community participation, community involvement, community empowerment) (Adams et al., 2020; Mills et al., 2020; Pappa et al., 2020; Unadkat & Farquhar, 2020; WHO, 2022a). Through taking action in terms of providing self-care, we have the potential to not only strengthen educational institutions in an effort to maximise efficient use of domestic resources for learning, but also to create innovations within the educational sector. By introducing mental health approaches, we can improve access to education and hybrid ways of being between educational systems and the personal private sphere.

Maintaining routines in everyday life, limiting social media consumption in terms of COVID-19 news, and the management of one's own thoughts in regard to "will I or will I not become infected" are known psychological strategies for maintaining our collective psychological health during the pandemic (Norcross & Phillips, 2020). This will effectively reduce doomsday anxiety. Mindfulness have had known effects of positive development for humans during stress and many researchers, particularly within the psychology discipline, have reminded us about the importance of practicing this on a daily basis (Diener, 2009; Geller, 2017; Norcross & Vandenbos, 2018; Norcross & Phillips, 2020). However, practicing mindfulness is often times disrupted during a global crisis since "moments of happiness and other positive emotions occur every day even during a pandemic, but we often fail to absorb and internalize them" (Norcross & Phillips, 2020, p. 61), resulting in a loss of positive emotions during such challenging times. In other fields, such as education, some researchers argue that due to women being higher represented in spheres of higher education such as teaching and service, the demands for these women to alter their way of working, thus causing an increased amount of stress, are greater than that of their male counterparts (Dingel et al., 2021).

From these premises, in this chapter we will explore self-care and strategies of wellbeing in academia through the voices of three parents in two nations in both the northern and southern hemisphere (Australia and Sweden) through lived experience of COVID-19 and hybrid ways of being. We engage with autoethnographic narratives, arranged into case studies, to provide personal reflections regarding ways of managing our mental health during the pandemic. The autoethnographic approach seeks to describe, understand, and transmit our personal experiences in order to make sense of them (Ellis, 2004) as well as illustrate similarities and also differences between them. We will do this through applying a phenomenological approach. Next, we will describe our theoretical approach, before introducing the narratives, as described by voices 1, 2, and 3.

Theoretical approach

In the following text three life stories will be presented. Stories about academics' everyday life during a pandemic, when work and private life increasingly flow together in an infinite and ongoing process. What experiences are central for the person to handle the two-dimensional new life situation and which strategies are used to create individual wellbeing and balance between work-life and family?

We have been inspired by the reflective life world philosophical theory with traditions of phenomenology and hermeneutics (Dahlberg, Dahlberg et al., 2008; Dahlberg, Ellingsen et al., 2019). The phenomenological approach is about describing and understanding the world the way it is experienced by humans; how meanings are created in this world and how humans relate to the world. Life worlds are always individual and unique, as well as contextual. Everyone experiences and creates meaning from an individual perspective, at the same time the individual life world exists in relation to the common world. How people achieve wellbeing and meaningfulness in this study refers to the concept of self-care, which is an individual and unique process depending on the person's life situation and personal experiences. Hence, self-care is here the central phenomenon.

During the analytical process we try to understand and grasp the essence of the phenomena and its essential meanings, which we present through three themes. Applying themes is compatible with phenomenology in that it offers the possibility to focus on the research participants' subjective experiences and also their individual sense-making (Braun & Clarke, 2019). Thus, it is an open, descriptive, and reflective process where the researcher alternates between the whole, the part, and the whole again (Dahlberg et al., 2008). We begin by allowing three voices to emerge (two in Sweden and one in Australia). The voices share intimate details of the whole–part–whole around self-care strategies through the use of visual photos as prompts. Each voice was asked to reflect on two to three photos to allow recall. The photos provide a type of implicit recall of experience to show meaningfulness within our COVID-19 experiences. A key consideration is that, as authors, we were based in two different countries and had two different sets of government regulations. As authors, we came together and discussed our reflections from the photos, prompting shared understandings of experience. After each voice is shared, we discuss the practicalities and implications of work-life balance with COVID-19. We draw on the key themes within and across the shared reflections to provide a joint understanding of overcoming the personal and professional blur to create different ways of academic work during COVID-19 and self-care.

Voice 1 narrative

In Melbourne, we have had numerous lockdowns with different levels of remote learning expected. In the second lockdown, schools and early childhood services were closed, as well as playgrounds. Parents were expected to work full time while also looking after children. It has become normal to see children and animals in online meetings. I would use my phone more to allow me to supervise my daughter's activities while also being able to participate in meetings. The new way of working also allowed me to have more time with my daughter – lunch as well as before and after work. This meant we could enjoy each other's company and also finish work at a better time (without commuting) to allow an afternoon walk together or activity outside. My daughter's favorite activity was picking flowers.

Image 7.1 Daily walks around the block.

In other Melbourne lockdowns, I was given the status of being "an essential worker". This meant I could send my daughter to the early childhood setting. During this time the work-life balance became even easier. I enjoyed getting my daughter ready in the morning and also picking her up from the early learning centre. Since I was still working from home and the early learning centre was close by, I had extra time in my day to balance things as I did not have the commute into the office. The extra time saved allowed me to exercise, plan my work better, and also cook healthier meals for our family. We noticed that since we were able to be home, our health was also improving.

When the COVID-19 situation started to ease, we were expected back in the office a couple of days a week. The flexibility of still allowing us to work from home was good. It allowed us to have balance with family while also being productive. The days that we were in the office were for meetings, to allow a sense of collaboration and networking.

Image 7.2 Eating healthy and exercise.

Image 7.3 Exercising together.

However in the current wave of Omicron we are again working from home (now in our third year). The benefits of having the flexibility of working from home largely outweigh the time wasted having to get ready for work and commuting to the office. Then it is the everyday time wasters of going into the office – traffic, finding a car park, not being able to find things in the office that are easily accessible at home. At home I have been able to create a study with a standing desk and everything that I need around me. I know I am in a safe environment.

The personal and professional blur 109

I am hesitant about the return to the office following the current wave. Instead I will continue to advocate for hybrid ways of working that allows opportunities for parents to really balance family and work. I do not think I could go back to spending five days in the office! The problem is I know all of the wasted time that could be better used towards wellbeing and family. For example, in the morning, my daughter and I practice yoga when we wake up. We are refreshed and focused for the day. On the days that I will need to get into the office, we would not have time for this activity. Likewise, I am able to finish earlier in the day (5 pm) and just leave my study to be present in the family. I do not need to hop in the car, drive through peak hour traffic and think about all of the home tasks I have to do. Instead we can have a relaxing walk before making dinner.

Another benefit for me in regards to wellbeing has been the use of online deliveries. This has meant limited trips to shops. I order everything online and being able to work from home means that everything is delivered straight to my front door. I am able to undertake online shopping when it suits me and have things delivered for my convenience. Prior to the pandemic, I would have gone to the grocery shops, clothes shops, and shopping centres. Now being able to save time through online deliveries also gives me better satisfaction that I am in control and I have more time to think about research and teaching during my work hours without having to think about what I will cook for dinner.

In 2022 as part of hybrid modes of working, I am also trying to implement a number of strategies to support wellbeing. This includes the shortening of meetings to 30 minutes. Meetings need an outcome and actions. I am trying to also schedule out "working time" that allows me to spend extended periods on tasks. For the first time in my life, I am starting to understand how I can manage my time effectively and be productive. I also plan in elements of wellbeing across my day. This is also part of a focus to continue to develop and strengthen resiliency throughout the pandemic.

Voice 2

Sweden's quite unique response to the COVID-19 pandemic coupled with children's duty of attendance in school meant that we never had to combine home-schooling with working from home. This meant that when I started my new job as a lecturer in early childhood education in March 2021, I was able to work from home. For the first year, this was in many ways, quite a relief. My eldest son, who is nine, doesn't have after-school care, so his routine is to come home direct after school around 2 pm, walk our family dog and then make himself an afternoon snack. Working from home meant that I could now be here when he came home; albeit I was not always available immediately, he knew I was there. It also meant no travel time in the morning, resulting in slower, more harmonious mornings for the whole family.

My new employer provided me with any necessary equipment for a successful home office, from laptop, big screen, keyboard, to adjustable laptop stand, to ensure that I could work in an ergonomically correct position. However, most of the time I worked on my laptop and even though we do have an actual home office, my work somehow just seemed to spill into every corner of my life. As the lines between my personal and professional life became more and more blurred, as did the boundaries of *where* and *when* to work. Work would encompass more or less all of my life and the "office" never really closed. For better or worse, this also meant that if a child had to stay at home due to illness, I could carry on working, whilst also caring for him. The sensation of safety and comfort in being able to combine my role as academic and as a mother, came to be a strategy of wellbeing in itself and this hybrid way of being soon became a pillar in our family life.

Blending my private self and professional self resulted somehow in an emergence of a newer, more relaxed me. This was, at least in part, due to much of the guilt I had previously felt for working more than full time when also being a mother evaporated, but also due to the new possibilities within my time management. At lunch, I could fit in a gym session at home, cook a healthy meal for myself, and take a relaxing shower, all in 60 minutes.

Image 7.4 Feeling good after a lunch-time workout.

The personal and professional blur 111

Often times I would start my day at 5 am, work on my laptop by candlelight, in my pajamas, and get two hours of work done before the children even awoke. This kind of time management allowed me then to spend precious time with my youngest for instance, when he returned from after school care. One example was spring 2021, when we would go out and pick flowers, which he would work with making bunches for the dinner table, whilst I finished up emailing and other tasks.

Having always been a holistic health-oriented kind of person, I effectivised my working day and after having seen my kids off to school, I'd settle in for morning meetings or assessments. Having no travel time or any logistics to

Image 7.5 Making table decorations in the early afternoon.

consider meant two things however. On the one hand it meant that I had more time in the morning to see my kids off to school and to tidy up the home after breakfast and morning routines. On the other hand, it meant that I lost some of the natural movement that would otherwise be integrated into my day, like walking to and from the commuter train, the station to the university and so on. Reflecting on this, I decided that I would continue "walking to work" and imagined myself, as I left in the morning to take Vincent on his morning stroll, walking to the "office". Returning then, after our walk and having fed and played with him for a bit, I would consider my working day to have begun. One tremendous benefit of this was that this companion of mine had company all day long, every day.

Image 7.6 Walking to "the office" with Vincent the Shih T'zu.

Slowly things started to change, vaccines were widely distributed and the government started talking about lifting restrictions. During this time my university went through a restructuring of departments, leaving me with a new immediate manager. Equally supportive as the previous one, I was able to continue my work as before for quite some time. As we moved from level red to level yellow to what we called level "lime", however, we were asked to slowly return to work and with wary steps, I did just that.

Journeying forward, I take with me this newfound knowledge of hybrid ways of being and I continue to practice the little things in my every day: the morning walks, the lunch-time movement and exercise, the healthy eating and the slower tempo. Waking at 5 am, however, has manifested itself as the most significant strategy for me. This time in the morning, before the world wakes, has become my happy place. I do my best work during this time and it sets me up for the rest of the day, providing me with energy, positivity, and a sensation of hope. Perhaps it is the silence, perhaps it is being awake every morning to see the sunrise and knowing that it will keep doing so, day after day and that gives me hope. Hope for a happier, healthier future for all of us.

Voice 3

In Spring 2021, the pandemic restrictions in Swedish society were at their height, and the government decided that a maximum of eight people were allowed at general gatherings. That was when I had to defend my dissertation. In Sweden, this is a public ceremony that usually takes place at the university and often ends with a big party.

However, due to the circumstances, it was only possible to conduct the defense online. Both the opponent and the examining committee attended digitally, and the auditorium was empty. Although my dreams did not match well with reality, I experienced it as the only option, and I reconciled with the circumstances: it was still a joyful and memorable day.

Now, I had received a doctoral degree and was full of enthusiasm for my new professional role as a senior lecturer. However, it turned out that returning to a regular job entirely at a distance was not as easy and motivating as I had expected. I missed meeting my colleagues and students in person. This resulted in that I, who am usually a social person, felt depressed and partially lost my motivation.

I was always at home with a computer in the middle of the kitchen table. For me, it was obvious that work was in progress. It turned out not to be so apparent for my 14-year-old son and my 10-year-old daughter, however, who suddenly wanted to be transported and picked up from various after-school activities. They wanted to talk, get help fixing snacks, and so on. Another factor was the email box that never ran out; a consequence of the pandemic seemed to be that emails were sent at all hours of the day and night because the normal circadian rhythm changed for many people.

Image 7.7 Defending my dissertation.

Initially I found this situation very frustrating and stressful. Work and leisure, weekdays and weekends merged into a single endless transport stretch, and I never felt that I had time to finish my tasks for work or have time for self-care. So, I slowly created new routines for a better balance between work and leisure both consciously and actively. I also decided to take advantage of the situation and create strategies for my own wellbeing as well as for my family, in this new hybrid way of working and being.

For me, this was initially very much a mental process, trying to see the benefits instead of the obstacles. Feeling the children's presence and conversations as something that became a positive part of my working day and gave me an opportunity for breaks and social interactions and to value this. When a child

Image 7.8 A lunch walk in the winter landscape.

calls, I have an opportunity to support my sometimes quite forgetful teenager with lost things like keys, the laptop, and so on. But the most important thing is to be there for my children when life is tough or they are having a bad day. This contributed to an increased sense of wellbeing both for myself and for my children.

    I also started taking regular lunch walks in daylight and soon noticed that I became happier and more alert. In addition, I also have lunch walks with

Image 7.9 Time for relaxing.

friends and sometimes with colleagues, and the ideas often flowed during these walks.

Some days I took a needed break from the monotonous computer work and stretched my body, relaxing and just breathing. Gradually, I also developed strategies to achieve a better balance between work and leisure. For me, it became important to set an end time for the working day and not to work on the weekends. I also limited reading the constant flow of emails to a couple of times a day.

I only have a five-minute walk to my office at the university, so when the restrictions were lifted to some extent, I often split my workday and was at the office half the day and at home the other half. In doing so, I could benefit from both environments. I found a good balance that suited my needs for both social interaction and supporting my family, and my work again felt meaningful.

Today, the restrictions have been lifted in Sweden, and there is a gradual decline in being physically at university. Of course, this is not something that happens automatically and without resistance. We have built up a new normal situation for two years. Personally, I am very much looking forward to spending more time at the university. I am convinced that we have learned a lot from the pandemic, which hopefully can contribute to a more flexible and

The personal and professional blur 117

hybrid way of being and working in the future – to a greater extent based on personal needs, resulting in increased wellbeing and a more valid life.

Discussion and conclusion

In this chapter we have shared personal reflections through offering collective autoethnographic narratives about hybrid ways of being, where we demonstrate the personal and professional blur during a global pandemic. By narrating the voices of three parents, who are also women academics, across two cultural contexts, Sweden and Australia, we describe our everyday lives in the context of work–life balance and strategies of wellbeing during the pandemic. We do this in an effort to broaden understanding about wellbeing and the strategies we have implemented during this time of crisis. Situated across two different cultural contexts, we illustrate similarities and differences between these strategies, shedding light on the importance of caring for one's own mental health and the importance of time management.

Across the reflections, key themes emerge for the three authors. The first theme is around wellbeing and how new strategies were implemented with movement and health when working from home. This included trying to reschedule and fit in activities during the workday or immediately before or after work. Within the reflections, part of this also allowed acknowledgement as women that it was ok to take and make time for themselves to help support resiliency and continued wellbeing as the pandemic continued.

Another theme to emerge was the blurring over time between professional and personal boundaries as working from home continued, meaning roles, relationships, and processes were continually being re-established and renegotiated. Prior to COVID-19 there was clear separation of work and home environments, which also influenced parenting and household routines (such as dropping children off at school and evening, or extra-curricular activities) and time management. COVID-19 provided a space for this to be reflected upon and also explore elements of closeness and distance within the blurring. These blurrings were also dependent on time. For example, there was always a shifting nature of the COVID-19 stage and the amount of time the academic would spend in the home or in the workplace. As such, the balancing was ongoing and required continual negotiations as the environment changed and continues to change. The constant changing landscape may also explain why health and wellbeing became a focus to help support resiliency to deal with continual changes.

Another theme to emerge was around the monotonous work of computers and meetings and how each academic navigated this space. Given that academics could only communicate online, time in front of screens and online meetings also became an issue. This led to fatigue and the academics trying to create new strategies to navigate better ways to manage this fatigue. Thus, a level of self-care was evident to support new developments and ways of working within online environments and better management of time.

Through the three narratives presented, the essence of the concept of self-care in this context emerges as an individual journey where each person assumes control of her situation through acceptance and also by prioritising her own mental and physical health in various ways. When boundaries are blurred between work and leisure, self-care become tools for dealing with change and with new challenges, through being creative and allowing new solutions which in turn may contribute to a balance between work and family life. Overall, the lesson learned by the academics show resiliency in adapting to change. Change is again occurring as hybrid and return to office models are implemented. This means negotiations and further understandings of work-life balance within the academy. It is hoped that lessons can be learned from the pandemic but also promote better supports for working parents to support work-life balance within academia.

Note

1 Food that provides a nostalgic or sentimental value to someone (Merriam-Webster 2011).

References

Adams, M., Chase, J., Doyle, C., & Mills, J. (2020). Self-care planning supports clinical care: Putting total care into practice. *Prog Palliat Care, 28*, 305–307.

Braun, V., & Clarke, V. (2019). Thematic analysis. *Handbook of Research Methods in Health Social Sciences*. Hoboken, NJ: Springer: 843–860. doi:10.1007/978-981-10-5251-4_103. ISBN 978-981-10-5250-7

Dahlberg, H. K., Ellingsen, S., Martinsen, B., & Rosberg, B. (Red.). (2019). *Phenomenology in practice: Phenomenological research in a scandinavian perspective* (1st ed.). ISBN: 9789147113453.

Dahlberg, K., Dahlberg, H., & Nyström, M. (2008). *Reflective lifeworld research* (2nd ed.). Studentlitteratur.

Diener, E. (2009). *The science of wellbeing*. Springer.

Dingel, M., Nichols, M., Mejia, A., & Osiecki, K. (2021). Service, self-care, and sacrifice: A qualitative exploration of the pandemic university as a greedy institution. *ADVANCE Journal, 2*(3), 24814.

Geller, S. (2017). *A practical guide to cultivating therapeutic presence*. American Psychological Association.

Mills, J., Ramachenderan, J., Chapman, M., Greenland, R., & Agar, M. (2020). Prioritising workforce wellbeing and resilience: What COVID-19 is reminding us about self-care and staff support. *Palliative Medicine, 34*(9), 1137–1139. doi:10.1177/0269216320947966

Norcross, J. C., & Phillips, C. M. (2020). Psychologist self-care during the pandemic: Now more than ever. *Journal of Health Service Psychology, 46*(2), 59–63.

Norcross, J. C., & VandenBos, G. R. (2018). *Leaving it at the office: A guide to psychotherapist self-care* (2nd ed.). Guilford.

Pappa, S., Ntella, V., Giannakas, T., Giannakoulis, V. G., Papoutsi, E., & Katsaounou, P. (2020). Prevalence of depression, anxiety, and insomnia among healthcare workers during the COVID-19 pandemic: A systematic review and meta-analysis. *Brain, Behavior, and Immunity*. "Comfort food" (definition). Merriam-webster.com. Retrieved February 25, 2022.

Unadkat, S., & Farquhar, M. (2020). Doctors' wellbeing: Self-care during the covid-19 pandemic. *BMJ, 368*, m1150. doi:10.1136/bmj.m1150

World Health Organization. (2022a). *What do we mean by self-care?* Retrieved January 25, 2022, from www.who.int/reproductivehealth/self-care-interventions/definitions/en/

World Health Organization. (2022b). *WHO coronavirus (COVID-19) dashboard*. Retrieved January 25, from https://covid19.who.int/

8 Spaces to care and places to share

Fostering a sense of belonging during the global pandemic through digitally mediated activity

Donna Pendergast, Alison Sammel, Leonie Rowan, Mia O'Brien, Tracey McCann, Harry Kanasa, David Geelan, Beryl Exley, Catherine Dennett, and Sakinah Alhadad

No introduction required: COVID-19 arrives in Australia, 25 January 2020
On 25 January 2020, the first case of COVID-19 was confirmed in Australia and on 11 March, a global pandemic was declared. Reducing the spread of infection and *flattening the curve* became policy priorities across the nation. Hand washing, mask wearing, and social distancing practices were implemented, alongside compulsory isolation and quarantining, contact tracing and intra- and international border closures. For extended periods of time people were ordered into lockdown, with limited justifications for leaving home. Non-essential services – including universities – were directed to implement a range of adjustments and campuses closed as communities entered lockdown. The university sector implemented work-from-home and remote learning, rendering previously active workplaces silent and empty: a strange and unsettling new reality captured in Image 8.1 at the time when staff members were packing their work belongings and relocating for an extended but unknown length of time. University teachers, and the professional staff that support them, rapidly shifted online to what is now known as "emergency remote teaching" (Rapanta et al., 2020, p. 927).

While every staff member shared the uncertainty of what was ahead, each had a unique experience depending upon their circumstances. The loss of partitions or boundaries between areas such as home and work, home and school, leisure and work, and, fundamentally, between the public and the private, created a distinctive cultural shift (Pendergast & Deagon, 2021). For some, working from home meant working in isolation. For others it meant struggling to find a private space in a house crowded with others (and their pets). Some experienced challenges with technology and infrastructure. Others had substantial parent and carer responsibilities which could not be outsourced. Some were thrust into the responsibility of supporting their children and teenagers to learn from home. Others faced food shortages and

DOI: 10.4324/9781003315797-11

Spaces to care and places to share 121

Image 8.1 Going, going, gone. Campuses emptied and offices abandoned during the first phase of lockdown in Queensland, commencing 16 March 2020.

the brewing threat of the loss of income whilst our university working and learning spaces were desolate.

Thus, as the world grappled with COVID-19, a second crisis emerged – the mental health pandemic. The detrimental effects of COVID-19 generated enormous mental health challenges across all age groups and professions, and systems struggled to cope (Choi et al., 2020). University teachers and professional staff were not immune to this (Maqsood et al., 2021), but were also

122 *Donna Pendergast et al.*

concurrently coping with supporting university students who were experiencing declining mental health (Baker et al., 2021; Kim et al., 2021).

During the first year of the pandemic, the Australian university sector experienced an estimated revenue fall of $1.8 billion (AUD) and 17,300 jobs were lost especially as a consequence of international student load (Jackson, 2021). This placed further pressure on disrupted university staff, some of whom felt their jobs and livelihood were at risk. Scull et al. (2020, p. 497) described the university sector in Australia as being "hit hard", with federal government decisions meaning that it was excluded from financial support available to other sectors. Tough economic decisions were made, procedures were rationalised and budgets were trimmed. It was a time of constant, unrelenting uncertainty and change and we struggled individually and collectively, with this forced and unwelcome transition. Staying well and healthy in this space required considerable effort and as we returned to campus, we discovered the familiar had become unfamiliar (see Image 8.2) and the unfamiliar was to become familiar.

Image 8.2 The strange becomes familiar: unfamiliar accessories, practices, and signage multiply.

We acknowledge that even something as seemingly universal as a pandemic is ultimately experienced in unique and particular ways by various individuals and groups. We therefore have adopted a visual methodology to capture the disparate experiences of multiple people, as we journeyed – together, and alone, connected, and apart – from disruption to uncertainty and beyond. Our focus throughout is on the ways we attempted to create or recreate opportunities for connection and belonging between the members of our work community. We share our digitally mediated strategy to fostering a sense of belonging amidst the pandemic. Alongside the digital disruption in higher education, we collectively, on a grassroots level, expand beyond typical digital boundaries, innovating and augmenting experiences of community and belonging through the digital world.

Seeing is part of believing: visual methodology and the goals of this chapter

Collecting visual artefacts as part of a research project is a well-established practice (see Pink, 2009). Researchers conducting ethnography or case studies, for example, have long embraced visual texts for their capacity to enhance "the richness" of other forms of qualitative or quantitative data, allowing researchers to exceed the boundaries of the written word when attempting to capture and communicate insights in different, and often challenging ways (Exley & Cottrell, 2012).

To adopt a visual methodology, however, is to go well beyond the simple inclusion of visual artefacts within a larger, more orthodox data set. Rather, it is to use the visual to shape questions and present findings, demanding that we seek knowledge from what people see and describe, and then connect this to explorations of how experiences are felt, heard, and embodied. One picture may be worth one thousand words, but those words still need to be read or seen. Visual methodologies give centre stage to these ways of speaking and ways of listening. Researchers such as Sarah Pink describe the power of "sensory ethnography", which brings "audiences close to other people's multisensory experiences, knowing, practice, memories and imaginations" (Pink, 2009, p. 132) and allows for the generation of "empathetic understandings" (2009, p. 134).

In this chapter we use the sensitivities and awareness encouraged by visual ethnographers to provide snapshots of various moments in time experienced by the people in our work community during the pandemic. We present *still life* images offering proof that there was, indeed, still life in our community, despite our circumstances.

Each visual artefact included in this chapter has been selected by members of the writing team because of the way it represents some aspect of wellbeing and resonated with our experience. We make no claim that our visuals can either capture or unproblematically represent "the truth" of our situations. Rather, like Pink (2009), we recognise that working with visual texts facilitates a

124   *Donna Pendergast et al.*

destabilisation of traditional notions of meaning as transparent and truth as clearly discernible while allowing new ways of understanding individuals. We present insights into experiences of isolation and fear, hope and confusion, risk taking and joy. The visuals included acknowledge the way any experience involves the intersection of the physical and material, the emotional and the social, connections and disconnections on people's sense of reality, and we focus on the ways in which a sense of belonging was desired, imagined, proffered and re-shaped. Through this process we reflect and contribute to a wider body of literature that explores the challenges of belonging and self-care in a time of pandemic.

Belonging and self-care

Sense of belonging

Sense of belonging is a complex concept that "is not seen as a permanent state but is variable and changeable across contexts, time and under different conditions" (Dewhurst et al., 2020, p. 18). This is extended by Somers (1999) who describes belonging as:

> [T]he need to be, and perception of being involved with others at differing interpersonal levels . . . which contributes to one's sense of connectedness (being part of, feeling accepted, and fitting in), and esteem (being cared about, valued and respected by others), while providing reciprocal acceptance, caring and valuing to others.
>
> (p. 3)

Having a positive sense of belonging is important because it serves as a protective factor in times of stress and is important for psychological wellbeing. Indeed, fostering a sense of belonging in communities, including that of workplaces, can have significant implications not only for mitigating a sense of exclusion, social isolation, and even preventing depression, but also supports one's sense of self as well as work performance (Cockshaw & Shochet, 2010; Waller, 2021). Garvis et al. (2022) provide an accessible interpretation of a literature review conducted by Lähdesmäki et al. (2016) which examined 67 articles with a focus on sense of belonging in a research context. Five themes emerged from the analysis, as presented in Table 8.1.

This framework serves as a useful way of reflecting upon the various themes of belonging.

Self-care

Self-care refers to intentional actions that foster protective factors for both individual and collective wellbeing (Riegel et al., 2021). Self-care can change the behaviour and frames of mind that are actioned with the conscious intention to build resilience, confidence, self-reliance and a sense of wellbeing. It is the

Spaces to care and places to share 125

Table 8.1 The Concept of Belonging – Five Themes Emerging from the Literature.

Belonging themes	Explanation of the theme
Spatiality	This sense of belonging is underpinned by place attachments and spatiality, for example offices, geographical places, homes, suburbs etc. Individuals typically feel a sense of belonging to multiple spaces both concurrently and sequentially.
Intersectionality	The collision and/or alignment of different formations of belonging, e.g., woman and academic, religion and ethnicity, employee and family.
Multiplicity	The notion of belonging constantly changing over time and being added to over time, and perceived as situational and constantly negotiated.
Materiality	This captures the relationship of people's interactions with their physical surroundings, and the social capital involved, and how this contributes to their sense of community and sense of belonging.
Non-belonging	This is a sense of being excluded, marginalised, not-being something. This might refer, for example, to a sense of faking it or being an imposter in the academy.

Source: Adapted from Lähdesmäki et al. (2016)

capacity to activate these ways of thinking and being as an agentic response to challenging times. The World Health Organization (2020) views self-care as the ability of individuals, families, and communities to act with self-reliance, empowerment, autonomy, personal responsibility, and self-efficacy towards good health and wellbeing. While there are many models of self-care in the current literature, they can be helpfully synthesised as comprising four inter-related dimensions that entail: self-care activities, self-care behaviours, self-care context, and self-care environment (El-Osta et al., 2019).

Aligned with these dimensions, a systematic review of self-care research (Matarese et al., 2018) noted that self-care refers primarily to three interrelated components – activity, capability, and process. Self-care activity refers to the learned and con-sciously performed physical, mental, social, and spiritual activities performed agentically by an individual towards specific goals. Self-care capability refers to individual abilities that are directed towards affirming or improving wellbeing (such as consolidating one's confidence or reframing pessimism with optimism). Self-care process, while often used explicitly with reference to health contexts, refers more broadly to self-management strategies and engagement in affirming psychosocial experiences. Across the literature there is a firm emphasis on the cen-tral role of individual intention and agency, considered to be a defining feature and distinguishing characteristic of self-care (El-Osta et al., 2019; Riegel et al., 2021).

In organisational contexts such as health, education, and the provision of care, the implementation of self-care awareness and practices has been linked to gains in wellbeing, positive affect, and self-compassion, and there is strong evidence that explicit self-care practices mediate the potentially negative impact of social and environmental stressors (Neimeyer & Taylor, 2019; Shapiro et al., 2007).

126 *Donna Pendergast et al.*

Of high relevance to our context, teacher self-care has been identified as a central factor in teacher pedagogical wellbeing. Higher levels of self-care can positively influence teachers' capacity to sustain quality pedagogical practice (Murphy et al., 2020).

The practices reported in this chapter were directed at affirming self-care practices across our school community. Our hope was that this would build both *individual* and *collective* experiences of self-reliance, efficacy, empowerment, autonomy, both personal and social responsibility as we worked collectively and collaboratively through the challenges of the pandemic. We also acknowledge the potential risks of adding to a sense of non-belonging, a sense of being excluded or marginalised.

We work in a school of 60+ academic and professional staff with an annual load of more than 3,000 full-time students. In March 2020 we welcomed a new intake of approximately 1,000 students to our programs. Within weeks, the declaration of the COVID-19 global pandemic and rapid shift to emergency education meant students and staff were in home lockdown. Our school had a long-established Wellbeing Committee (Image 8.3) in place, framing our culture of care. Some of our specific initiatives included

- establishing the EPS Work Family Facebook private group,
- weekly virtual staff forums, highlighting personal achievements and pre-recorded performances from the school music group #harrymademedoit, and entertainment such as quizzes and sing-a-longs,

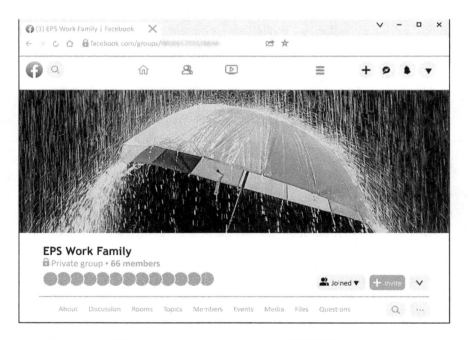

Image 8.3 School of Education and Professional Studies (EPS) Wellbeing Committee image, used for the EPS Work Family Facebook Group.

Spaces to care and places to share 127

Image 8.4 Flattening the curve – no probllama.
Artist: Tracey McCann

- establishing a virtual walking club,
- hosting a weekly trivia evening,
- following the adventures of our school mascot, Stuart T. Llama, represented in Image 8.4, which was gifted at and then spirited away from a School Christmas event generating much speculation about his subsequent whereabouts and rumours of nefarious activity.

This chapter will share a selection of these activities and consider how they enabled self-care and a sense of belonging to flourish.

Together, apart: the ritual of weekly virtual forums

Experiencing comfort and contentment during our online meetings allowed us to individually develop our own sense of belonging. This experience was unique to each person and each meeting. During the meetings, school staff members were conscious of reducing the perception of pressure or judgement associated with participation and thus avoiding the accidental construction of non-belonging. Individuals chose their level of participation and there was shared talk about the understanding that the intersectionality of work/life

128 Donna Pendergast et al.

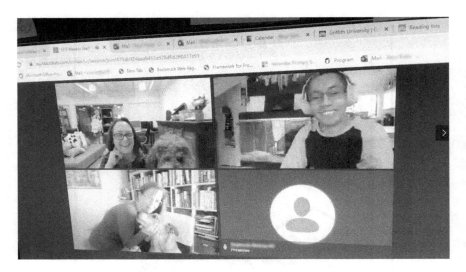

Image 8.5 It's okay to turn your camera on: creating safe collegial spaces.

varied for everyone during the lockdown journey. During the online meetings (see Image 8.5), a conscious attempt was made to preserve solitude within this collective space. Individuals did not have to be visible and smile and wave; individuals could be invisible and listen, or invisible and tune-out. Individuals who did not have the time or emotional energy to put on a brave face and pretend they could be engaged were not forced into a situation of toxic belonging. What was offered was a sense of fun, playfulness, and a gentle invitation to engage.

A pet-friendly space

Various strategies were used to offer engagement and to maximise the chance that people would feel connection to another person, or another place. One successful strategy was the introduction and connection with the more-than-human world we live with. The human brain has evolved from and for connections to natural systems (Sammel, in press) and the desire for connection is not limited to humanity. Australia has one of the highest pet ownership rates in the world, as there are 29 million registered pets to a human population of 25 million (Animal Medicines Australia, 2019). The *pet effect*, that is, living with a non-human companion, improves moment-to-moment mental wellbeing, long-term psychological and cardiovascular health, physical fitness, and immune system functioning (Smith, 2012). By including and greeting our non-humans we love and live with, a space was considerately and kindly made to welcome people into participating in ways that allowed happiness to

Spaces to care and places to share 129

Image 8.6 Where in the world is Stuart T. Llama, and what are those flowers he's smelling?

authentically emerge. One participant who does not have any household pets stated how much pleasure she derived from everyone else sharing their more-than-human world. Others were invited into the conversation through a hastily built, pet-related online quiz including questions about the names of various popular culture pets, and songs about dogs. In subsequent sessions the animal theme was extended to include those who did not own pets. We invited our participants to join a game of "Where in the World is Stuart T. Llama?", trying to identify the location of a wandering School mascot who appeared (through photoshopped wizardry) on places as diverse as football fields, musical theatre productions, and in multiple movies and artworks. Stuart was also spotted lurking in various pieces of shrubbery (see Image 8.6), providing links to the outdoors at a time when we spent far too much of each day inside.

For those not previously closely connected by physical space or job alignment, the virtual platform provided a new space and opportunities for connection. Several small groups of professional staff began meeting together online at a regular time each week, knowing that some members of the group were living alone. The groups formed a new sense of community that has continued past the lockdown period. There was also a greater sense of connectedness across the school, built from the insights that staff discovered about each other and knowledge about their lives that reached well beyond the professional. For example, one professional staff member noted with some surprise and delight that she "never realised that our Head of School actually walks dogs!"

Music matters

A regular feature of our weekly meetings was musical performances. Our "band" #harrymademedoit (*Harry Made Me Do It*, also known as #hmmdi), was born out of friendly intercampus musical rivalry prior to the pandemic, but quickly evolved into a collaboration to provide entertainment at the end-of-year school function. While the original intent was to place our spatiality (i.e., different home campuses) in opposition with one another, our overall sense of belonging to the School resulted in our merger and an agreement to perform semi-regularly (or at least annually) at whole-of-school functions.

Arranging a time and a location for all to be physically present for rehearsals proved challenging, which meant Image 8.7 records both our debut performance and the first time we had all played in the same place. For our debut performance there was a three-song set list: *Top of the World* (Carpenter & Bettis, 1973), Olivia Newton-John's version of *Let Me Be There* (Rostill, 1973), and *Crocodile Rock* (John & Taupin, 1972). We agonised over the playlist to ensure the songs were familiar, had a positive theme, and were boppy enough to encourage the audience to dance. Image 8.7 shows us with our red feather

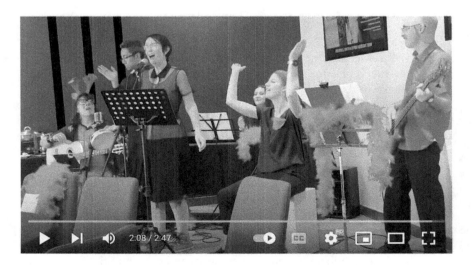

Image 8.7 HMMDI's debut performance: AKA everything is better with a boa.

boas, a clothing element to unify us as a band, and the joy on our faces shows the "buzz" we get from performing live . . . and just being able to be together to create music indicative of the materiality of the sense of belonging that was established within the band. This was when the band was officially named – under pressure, our lead singer blurted out "We're Harry Made Me Do It" – a respectful acknowledgement of the lead role one of our band played in bringing us together, regardless of the wide gaps in our various musical talents. The name stuck and the hashtag #harrymademedoit and its abbreviation #hmmdi were coined. Little did we know that individual practice and recording were to become a feature during the pandemic.

While we had anticipated that #hmmdi might not reconvene until the next whole of school event, our performances moved online once the pandemic hit (see Image 8.8).

Image 8.8 Moving our performances online – a shift from the physical to virtual space.

We were already comfortable communicating via email, practising individually and we had already semi-mastered (individually) the technology required for audio and video recording. Coordinating outfits continued as an established practice with a psychedelic, 60s vibe for *The 59th Street Bridge Song (Feelin' Groovy)* (Simon & Garfunkel, 1966) and classy all-black and shades for Peggy Lee's version of *Fever* (Cooley & Blackwell, 1956). The band members easily took this shift in spatiality in their stride but there were definitely moments when trying to synchronise five different audio tracks placed some demands on our joviality!

The work of the original band members produced some positive energy and a definite sense that music can connect people. The band members all enjoyed their chaotic catch ups and found a sense of purpose in contributing

132   *Donna Pendergast et al.*

to the broader school belonging agenda. A next step was to try and ensure that the joy captured in Image 8.7 was genuinely accessible to others and that non-belonging was minimised. Having established a very light-hearted tone for our performances (and emphasising that at least some of the members were very far away from being confident and regular performers), we began the process of trying to connect more people to the band either as regular performances, guest artists, or support crew. A call was put out for volunteers (which produced impressive ABBA impersonators) while others were tapped on the shoulder as guest performers. This provided staff with opportunities to communicate multiple parts of their identity and to be seen simultaneously in two different roles, that is, professional staff member or academic and singer, musician, or team member. This blurring of boundaries between the professional and the musical enhanced togetherness between colleagues who traditionally may have little recourse to interact as part of their duties (see Image 8.9).

To further extend the occasions for contribution, we invited people to contribute in ways that were not strictly musical. In our first online experience we pieced together a musical rendition of a re-worded version of *You Are My Sunshine* (Davis & Mitchell, 1940), which made reference to the power of our online connections and included pictures of things/people/places that our made our colleagues happy (see Image 8.9). A simple invitation via our Work Family Facebook Group generated 55 images.

In a later activity more than 13 staff provided vocal clips to our rendition of the Muppet Show classic song *Mahna Mahna* (Henson, 1995; Umiliani, 1969), which asked them to simply record a spoken version of themselves saying "Mahna Mahna" into their phones. Staff members were then invited to guess the voices in our weekly forum. This was one of our most successful audience participation activities.

And in a homage to our early performance of *Crocodile Rock* (John & Taupin, 1972), we invited staff to submit photos or videos of themselves (or their children, or their pets) dancing to the Elton John classic, which we edited into a new clip for the original sound track. Once again, the goal was to maximise pathways to connection during a time of liminality and, as the diverse visual artefacts in this section make clear, multiple voices were heard, multiple perspectives were seen, and new knowledge – about ourselves and each other – was created.

Weekly Friday evening trivia

Pre-COVID-19, a group of EPS staff met regularly to enter trivia competitions. When the lockdowns began, we were motivated to create our own version of trivia. The quizmaster created the approach using virtual tools, along with the character of the "Inquizitaur" (see Image 8.10) as the minotaur quizmaster, complete with labyrinth references in the weekly announcements and invitations placed in the EPS Work Family Facebook group.

Spaces to care and places to share 133

Image 8.9 Sunshine comes from many places: bringing others into a musical fold.

Image 8.10 Friday nights were not trivial.

The Friday night trivia events began with half an hour or so of drinks and conversations, which evolved into word games such as "Guess the animal I'm thinking of" using only yes/no answers, and variants such as "Guess the band or musical artist". Partners, families, and pets of EPS staff were welcome, and family teams joined in. Some evenings featured virtual wine tastings or cocktail recipe sharing, or themed hat or fancy-dress evenings. Questions canvassed a broad variety of general knowledge questions on the arts, sciences, politics, history, and a range of other topics. Each evening was made up of 20 questions, four of which were music questions, and these were usually themed in some way: ABBA, musicals, rock, and other variants.

Spaces to care and places to share 135

The trivia evenings provided materiality, albeit virtually, that offered opportunities to learn more about one another's knowledge, interests, and tastes, and provided a relaxing social end to each work week. The virtual space connected home spaces, and people and pets within, to one another. Conversations started through the trivia quiz continued in the weeks ahead. The intersectionality of belonging was keenly felt for those who participated in this way.

Postcards from around Australia – EPS Walk Around Australia

Another activity was connected to our Facebook community. At the start of lockdown, EPS colleagues were invited to join a private group on Facebook called EPS Work Family. The invitation to join the group provided a welcome and a reminder that the site was closed and "just for EPS folks", the aim being "to provide a space for us to stay connected during the physically distant but socially connected phase we're heading into". Another statement explained that this site was not to reproduce the "heap of things on FB and the 'gram and twitter", but to "share and support each other" and be "positive, affirming and collegial". Sixty-six members joined, made up of EPS academic and professional staff who typically work across three physical campuses spread 100 km apart and some of whom are employed in different divisions but work very closely with EPS staff.

A few weeks in, when the Government lockdown restrictions made an allowance so people could partake in outdoor exercise within a 5 km radius of their home and with household members only, one team member declared that the "EPS Work Fam walking holiday starts now" (see Image 8.11). In so doing, instructions were provided for logging places where people walked and distances travelled. The distances logged were added together. The initial intention was to walk across the three physical campuses to "visit" one another and say "hi". Activities of this ilk draw on process drama strategies and help to transform individuals from one place to another, in this case, from physically separated lockdowns to virtually connected walking tours. Bowell and Heap (2005, p. 59) describe process drama as a form of "applied theatre in which participants, together with the teacher, constitute the theatrical ensemble and engage in drama to make meaning for themselves". In process drama, participants are not learning and presenting lines from a pre-written script, rather they are scripting in the moment their own presentation as the narrative and tensions unfold in their own spaces and over time (Exley & Dooley, 2015). An internal audience replaces the external audience of the theatre so that participants are both the theatrical ensemble that creates the performance and the audience that receives it.

Facebook provided the spatiality for our *participatory culture* (Jenkins et al., 2009) to flourish, both in terms of bringing in the materiality of disparate physical (actual and virtual) surroundings. The Facebook group enabled individuals to engage in their own time frame, and still keep chronology in place by viewing, engaging, and responding to posts in time order. Another feature

136 Donna Pendergast et al.

Image 8.11 Walking together through thick and thin, even when we're walking alone.

of this online virtual affinity space is its capacity to transcend traditional limitations of textual dissemination, that is to capitalise upon the permeable boundaries where one text may hyperlink to another or virtual texts from different platforms can merge (Exley & Willis, 2016). In this way, Facebook extended the time and space available for individual reflection and self-care outside of the other activities on offer. We now share a small selection of posts where real names are replaced with pseudonyms, and for copyright reasons, images taken from the internet are replaced with similar images from our own photo library.

As it happened, the invitation to walk and share in the virtual journey across the three physical campuses was achieved in a matter of days – more people walked, and walked further, and chose to engage than expected. Another Facebook regular suggested that we keep walking and keep tallying and (virtually) circumnavigate Australia. There was enough interest, so the challenge began. One EPS member took the lead in mapping the journey and posting polls so participants could nominate the route and some attractions. Our (unspoken) shared goal was to collectively achieve something none of us could do alone during this period of time. In all, the virtual Walk Around Australia lasted 168 days, with a total of 597 posts added to our EPS Facebook site. Approximately 40 people viewed each post with approximately 12 comments and 5 reactions per post.

As these visual texts demonstrate, the line between the virtual and the real, between the walks we took when allowed out of home (initially within a 5 km radius), and the places we went in our imagination during that time, was beautifully blurred during this interactive activity. Reports of *steps taken* were interwoven with fictionalised accounts of what people did on their parallel virtual works. For example, in a post where our location was given as the Dreamworld theme park on the Gold Coast (see Image 8.12) and mention was made of the

Image 8.12 The idea to walk around Australia has been generated.

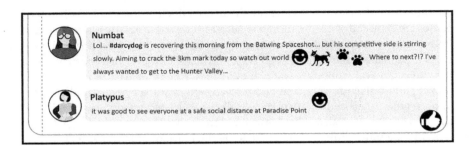

Image 8.13 #DARCYDOG adventure.

Batwing Spaceshot ride, one participant explained that her #darcydog was "recovering this morning from the Batwing Spaceshot . . . but his competitive side is stirring slowly" (see Image 8.13).

This form of participation made the imaginary space more real, accessible, and relevant. The playfulness of the process drama continued in varying intensities throughout the 168 days of the activity, as further shown in some of the images shared in this publication.

The community's sense of belonging was further enhanced via opportunities to exercise agency and share in the real decision making within this imaginary space. Polls were posted at semi-regular intervals so participants could help to construct the route and offer their own suggestion (see Image 8.14). Once participants offered up suggestions, they were then invited to take the "tour guide" role for the locations they had identified.

For example, if an individual offered that a particular location was their birthplace, or a place they had visited previously, they then identified what the collective group would see and do whilst on location. Sharing of connections and belonging, place attachments for individuals, and then collectively has the potential to enhance belonging.

Another foray into a shared process drama took place as we entered the Eyre Highway on the Nullarbor Plains. One participant recounted that on a recent trip across the Nullarbor Plain, her travel party played a round of golf. It's a quirky 18-hole par 72 golf course that spans 1,365 km, with each hole located near a township or roadhouse. We turned to imagining the playing of golf. If golf was mentioned in the posts, extra walking credits were added to the group tally. Walkers found their own unique and humorous way to continue and comment, as can be seen in Image 8.15.

One of our colleagues spent two periods of two weeks in hotel quarantine, a small room with no access to natural fresh air flow and without physical contact with the outside world. Hotel quarantine was a State Government initiative designed to isolate travellers who may have been exposed to the COVID-19 virus. The purpose was to monitor the traveller for signs of ill-health, and also to prevent

Image 8.14 Voting on the route to be walked.

these individuals from entering their communities until their risk of spreading COVID-19 had been determined. The purpose of the strategy notwithstanding, the risk was our colleague could slip into a sense of not belonging whilst locked in hotel quarantine. Virtual media and this belonging activity allowed her to maintain a sense of belonging and provide purpose (see Image 8.16).

A sad time occurred during our walking tour. One of our EPS walkers could walk no longer; our colleague passed away during lockdown. Gutted by our loss, and not having our usual ways of coming together in grief, we again turned to the virtual space and our mission (see Image 8.17). Some shared words in their own way in their own time. Others posted photos of our colleague, and of artefacts that drew attention to her memory. The sense of community and sense of belonging was not only just for entertainment and motivation to be physically active, it was also for the seriously sad work of grieving and supporting each other.

Finally, the day of the finale came – shared congratulations and shared celebrations! Finales are important for marking the achievement and marking the beginning of the end. It was permission to cease the role play, the disclosures of very personal histories such as places of birth and photos of physical (real) walks

140 Donna Pendergast et al.

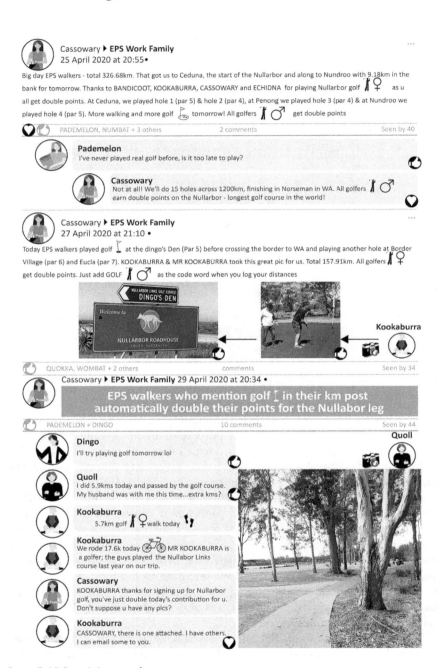

Image 8.15 Imagining together.

Spaces to care and places to share   141

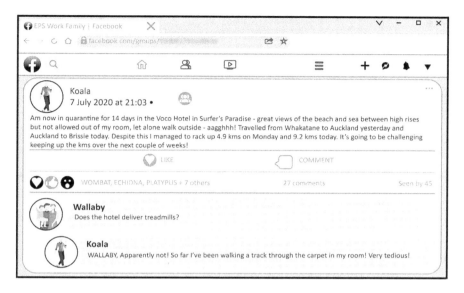

Image 8.16 Walking the room.

Image 8.17 One of our walkers could walk no longer.

Image 8.18 The finale – shared congratulations and shared celebrations.

and two- and four-legged family members. All good things come to an end and this was the end of the Walk Around Australia activity (see Image 8.18).

Life goes on

While the world's focus was on COVID-19, regular life events continued (see Image 8.19), albeit adjusted to comply with varying health regulations in force. Friends and family members were still undergoing treatment for other health issues. Babies were born. Tragic deaths occurred outside of COVID-19. Some of our community members took up new hobbies – painting, cooking, playing games – and found ways to stay connected with their families. Our children attended school, often at home under our watchful eye. Many milestone events were missed.

The rules and regulations around supporting others, celebrating, and mourning, missing rituals and routines, added to the mental anguish and social disconnect. Dropping a casual "Oh, by the way . . ." during a virtual trivia event seemed inappropriate and finding an outlet and a form of support was difficult. The need for self-care strategies was a priority for some. Finding a balance between performing our duties and taking care of our physical and mental wellbeing was openly discussed and encouraged. Anything from cooking classes to art classes, from garden design to furniture restoration. If you wanted to learn something in the safety of your own home, you could find it online and give it a go. And we supported each other to engage in what they needed, when they needed it.

Reflecting on our journey

It is sobering to reflect on these experiences and the varying levels of individual and collective engagement that occurred. The rituals, strategies, and practices

Spaces to care and places to share   143

Image 8.19 Life goes on.

presented here were highly emergent. While each started with a small number of staff driving an idea or initiative, all were responsive and reflexive to the ways in which other staff engaged, and each provided opportunities for all staff to fully participate.

Belonging through spatiality and materiality was enabled through consistent opportunities to connect to places of meaning and attachment. Belonging, as it turned out, through physically dispersed, virtually constructed means was not only possible, but it was also triumphant. Staff took turns to be "tour guide" in the Walk Around Australia, which for some was an opportunity to share places of interest from their birthplace or a place that remains familiar and dear. This made the activity personal and relational, and invited individuals to be a part of something that mattered for both themselves and their colleagues. Others found an opportunity to connect to the weekly Trivia night via their lounge room with snacks, beverages, and family members recruited as team

144 *Donna Pendergast et al.*

members. Many enjoyed the opportunity to feature works of art, funny photos, and favourite pets in weekly online virtual meetings. Staff found new ways to connect via their mutual enjoyment of music in the #harrymademedoit band. And mascot Stuart was to be found in the range of activities and adventures.

All of the strategies enabled an opening up of the ordinary, everyday ways of *being* in our school. They provided opportunities to include and value more expansive ways of being a member of the EPS community whilst ensuring staff felt included, agentic, and confident. In that way the strategies we've outlined here were intentional, making use of this space to build a positive sense of belonging, and in facilitating both *individual* and collective *experiences* of self-care through affirming self-reliance, efficacy, empowerment, autonomy, and responsibility. This was our preferred way of working collectively and collaboratively through the challenges of the pandemic.

The power of this relational, self-regulated engagement can be considered from the perspective of Matarese et al. (2018) three interrelated components of self-care – *activity, capability*, and *process*. In our digitally mediated space, *activities* were consciously performed, including physical, mental, social, and spiritual elements, agentically and with specific goals – whether to reach the next destination of the journey, compete to win the trivia, locate Stuart, or sing a song in a safe space. With respect to self-care *capability*, the activities were directed towards affirming and improving wellbeing. And finally, self-care *process* was evident with explicit reference to health contexts, such as the health benefits of the walking and self-management to the extent of participation that met individual needs and affirmed psychosocial experiences. In alignment with the literature, there was a firm emphasis on the central role of individual intention and agency, which is considered to be a defining feature and distinguishing characteristic of self-care (El-Osta et al., 2019; Riegel et al., 2021).

To be continued . . .

The rapidity and all-encompassing nature of the pandemic disrupted our lives; new ways of being were and remain unavoidable. At the time of writing this chapter some two years later, we do not yet have certainty of new ways. The promise of vaccines capable of silencing new viral variants has not yet been achieved, with continued outbreaks expected around the globe, making an end to the pandemic beyond the horizon (Kofman et al., 2021). Hence, we exist in a prolonged state of liminality, without an end in sight. The visual artefacts included in this chapter remind us that although we cannot see the end of "pandemic normality" nor even, in some cases, remember clearly all that came before, even in times of confusion and despair, small efforts to generate a sense of togetherness can have a major impact upon opportunities to feel and to experience an embodied sense of belonging. This effort continues today (see Image 8.20). The images we present are snapshots in time, and we do not know what experiences will come next. But we do know we are a place that values

Image 8.20 The authors, connected (in) still.

connectedness and sense of belonging. The snapshots serve as a reminder to all of us that when we place wellbeing, care-for-self, and care-for-others at the centre, connections are not only made possible, they are made beautiful.

References

Animal Medicines Australia. (2019). *Pets in Australia: A national survey of pets and people.* https://animalmedicinesaustralia.org.au/wp-content/uploads/2019/10/ANIM001-Pet-Survey-Report19_v1.7_WEB_low-res.pdf

Baker, C. N., Peele, H., Daniels, M., Saybe, M., Whalen, K., Overstreet, S., & Trauma-Informed Schools Learning Collaborative the New Orleans. (2021). The experience of covid-19 and its impact on teachers' mental health, coping, and teaching. *School Psychology Review, 50*(4), 491–504. http://doi.org/10.1080/2372966X.2020.1855473

Bowell, P., & Heap, B. (2005). Drama on the run: A prelude to mapping the practice of process drama. *Journal of Aesthetic Education, 39*(4), 58–69.

Carpenter, R., & Bettis, J. (1973). *Top of the world.* [Performed by The Carpenters]. A & M.

Choi, K. R., Heilemann, M. V., Fauer, A., & Mead, M. (2020). A second pandemic: Mental health spillover from the novel coronavirus (COVID-19). *Journal of the American Psychiatric Nurses Association, 26*(4), 340–343. http://doi.org/10.1177/1078390320919803

Cockshaw, W., & Shochet, I. (2010). The link between belongingness and depressive symptoms: An exploration in the workplace interpersonal context. *Australian Psychologist, 45*(4), 283–289. http://doi.org/10.1080/00050061003752418

Cooley, E., & Blackwell, O. (1956). *Fever.* [Performed by Peggy Lee, 1958].

Davis, J., & Mitchell, C. (1940). *You are my sunshine.* Decca.

Dewhurst, Y., Ronksley-Pavia, M., & Pendergast, D. (2020). Preservice teachers' sense of belonging during practicum placements. *Australian Journal of Teacher Education, 45*(11). https://ro.ecu.edu.au/ajte/vol45/iss11/2

146 *Donna Pendergast et al.*

El-Osta, A., Webber, D., Gnani, S., Banarsee, R., Mummery, D., Majeed, A., & Smith, P. (2019). The self-care matrix: A unifying framework for self-care. *Selfcare Journal, 10*(3), 38–56. https://selfcarejournal.com/wp-content/uploads/2019/07/El-Osta-et-al.-10.3.38–56.pdf

Exley, B., & Cottrell, A. (2012). Reading in the Australian curriculum English: Describing the effects of structure and organisation on multimodal texts. *English in Australia, 47*(2), 91–98.

Exley, B., & Dooley, K. (2015). Critical linguistics in the early years: Exploring language functions through sophisticated picture books and process drama strategies. In K. Winograd (Ed.), *Critical literacies and young learners: Connecting classroom practice to the common core* (pp. 128–143). Routledge.

Exley, B., & Willis, L.-D. (2016). Children's pedagogic rights in the web 2.0 era: A case study of a child's open access interactive travel blog. *Global Studies of Childhood, 6*(4), 400–413. http://doi/pdf/10.1177/2043610616676026

Garvis, S., Keary, A., Harju-Luukkainen, H., Yngvesson, T., & Pendergast, D. (2022). Creating a sense of belonging through self-care strategies in higher education. In N. Lemon (Ed.), *Healthy relationships in higher education* (pp. 55–75). Routledge. http://doi.org/10.4324/9781003144984-6

Henson, J. (Creator). (1995). *The Muppet show*. [TV Series]. The Muppets Studio; The Walt Disney Company.

Jackson, K. (2021, February 3). *17,000 Uni jobs lost to COVID-19*. Universities Australian Media Release. www.universitiesaustralia.edu.au/media-item/17000-uni-jobs-lost-to-covid-19/

Jenkins, H., Purushotma, R., Weigel, M., Clinton, K., & Robinson, A. J. (2009). *Confronting the challenges of participatory culture: Media education for the 21st century*. https://library.oapen.org/bitstream/handle/20.500.12657/26083/1004003.pdf

John, E., & Taupin, B. (1972). *Crocodile rock*. MCA; DJM.

Kim, L. E., Oxley, L., & Asbury, K. (2021). "My brain feels like a browser with 100 tabs open": A longitudinal study of teachers' mental health and well-being during the COVID-19 pandemic. *British Journal of Educational Psychology, 92*(1), 1–20. http://doi.org/10.1111/bjep.12450

Kofman, A., Kantor, R., & Adashi, E. Y. (2021). Potential COVID-19 endgame scenarios: Eradication, elimination, cohabitation, or conflagration? *Journal of the American Medical Association, 326*(4), 303–304. http://doi:10.1001/jama.2021.11042

Lähdesmäki, T., Saresma, T., Hiltunen, K., Jäntti, S., Sääskilahti, N., Vallius, A., & Ahvenjärvi, K. (2016). Fluidity and flexibility of "belonging": Uses of the concept in contemporary research. *Acta Sociologica, 59*(3), 233–247. http://doi.org/10.1177/0001699316633099

Maqsood, A., Abbas, J., Rehman, G., & Mubeen, R. (2021). The paradigm shift for educational system continuance in the advent of COVID-19 pandemic: Mental health challenges and reflections. *Current Research in Behavioral Sciences, 2*, Research Paper 100011. http://doi.org/10.1016/j.crbeha.2020.100011

Matarese, M., Lommi, M., Grazia, M., & Riegel, B. (2018). A systematic review and integration of concept analyses of self-care and related concepts. *Journal of Nursing Scholarship, 50*(3), 296–305. doi:10.1111/jnu.12385

Murphy, T. R., Masterson, M., Mannix-McNamara, P., Tally, P., & McLaughlin, E. (2020). The being of a teacher: Teacher pedagogical well-being and teacher self-care. *Teachers and Teaching, 26*(7–8), 588–601.

Neimeyer, G. J., & Taylor, J. M. (2019). Advancing the assessment of professional learning, self-care, and competence. *Professional Psychology: Research and Practice, 50*(2), 95–105. http://doi.org/10.1037/pro0000225

Pendergast, D., & Deagon, J. R. (2021). Home economics, the COVID-19 global pandemic and beyond. *International Journal of Home Economics, 14*(2), 2–15. www.ifhe.org/filead min/user_upload/e_Journal/vol_14_1/P1_Pendergast-Deagon.pdf

Pink, S. (2009). *Doing sensory ethnography.* Sage.

Rapanta, C., Botturi, L., Goodyear, P., Guárdia, L., & Koole, M. (2020). Online university teaching during and after the Covid-19 crisis: Refocusing teacher presence and learning activity. *Postdigital Science and Education, 2*(3), 923–945. http://doi.org/10.1007/s42438-020-00155-y

Riegel, B., Dunbar, S. B., Fitzsimons, D., Freedland, K. E., Lee, C. S., Middleton, S., Stromberg, A., Vellone, E., Webber, D. E., & Jaarsma, T. (2021). Self-care research: Where are we now? Where are we going? *International Journal of Nursing Studies, 116,* 103402. http://doi: 10.1016/j.ijnurstu.2019.103402

Rostill, J. (1973). *Let me be there.* [Performed by Olivia Newton-John]. Festival.

Sammel, A. (in press). Chapter 5. Connecting with local greenspaces: Wellbeing pedagogies for middle years students and teachers. In K. Main & S. Whatman (Eds.), *Health and wellbeing in the middle grades: Research for effective middle level education.* Information Age Publishing (IAP).

Scull, J., Phillips, M., Sharma, U., & Garnier, K. (2020). Innovations in teacher education at the time of COVID19: An Australian perspective. *Journal of Education for Teaching, 46*(4), 497–506. http://doi: 10.1080/02607476.2020.1802701

Shapiro, S. L., Brown, K. W., & Biegel, G. M. (2007). Teaching self-care to caregivers: Effects of mindfulness-based stress reduction on the mental health of therapists in training. *Training and Education in Professional Psychology, 1*(2), 105.

Simon, P., & Garfunkel, A. (1966). *59th street bridge song (Feelin' Groovy).* Columbia.

Smith, B. (2012). The 'pet effect': Health related aspects of companion animal ownership. *Australian Family Physician, 41*(6), 439–442. https://pubmed.ncbi.nlm.nih.gov/22675689/

Somers, M. D. (1999). *Development and preliminary validation of a measure of belongingness.* [Doctoral dissertation]. Temple University.

Umiliani, P. (1969). *Mah Nà Mah Nà.* Columbia.

Waller, L. (2021). Fostering a sense of belonging in the workplace: Enhancing well-being and a positive and coherent sense of self. In S. K. Dhiman (Ed.), *The Palgrave handbook of workplace well-being* (pp. 341–367). Palgrave Macmillan. http://doi.org/10.1007/978-3-030-30025-8_83

World Health Organization. (2020). *Economic and financing considerations of self-care interventions for sexual and reproductive health and rights Summary Report.* United Nations University Centre for Policy Research. https://apps.who.int/iris/bitstream/handle/10665/331195/WHO-SRH-20.2-eng.pdf

9 Ethical responsibility in the struggle between the public and the private space

Challenges and possibilities in teacher education during the pandemic

Marita Cronqvist

Introduction

During the pandemic, new and challenging conditions have characterised the academic work, for both students and educators (Dania, 2021). The previous physical meeting with the students had to be adapted to the conditions that the digital meeting entailed, which created uncertainty for both parties. In addition to this uncertainty and attempts to benefit from experiences of the forced digitalisation, social dimensions have received more attention in higher education (Farnell et al., 2021). Research indicates that self-compassion and wellbeing improve academic performance (Egan et al., 2021). The academic learning environment affects students' knowledge, skills, and values in a way that prepares them for their future professional practice and for their lives in general. Emotional experiences, self-care, and students' wellbeing during education affect their possibilities to learn and develop (Hagenauer et al., 2018) but is often underestimated (Roland & Jones, 2020; Tvedt et al., 2021). Additionally, educators influence students as role models and in reflective academic learning environments, with the tension between the public and private space must be handled ethically (Cronqvist, 2020).

In the educators' meeting with the preservice teachers, personality and self-awareness are of great importance for how they develop in the professional role (Schussler et al., 2010; Schussler & Knarr, 2013; Shapira-Lishinsky, 2011). Knowledge presupposes awareness and understanding of one's own life world (Merleau-Ponty, 2002/1945) and therefore, previous experiences, values, and attitudes need attention to be reflected and discussed in the education in order to stimulate and support learning. The boundary between the private and the professional thus ends up in a grey zone where it is not clear to distinguish one from the other. In order to meet preservice teachers in matters that concern the personal, teacher educators must be ethically responsible and willing to take discussions that mean that their own values and attitudes are put at the forefront (Bates et al., 2011). An important aspect of these meetings in teacher education is the preparation of preservice teachers so that they in turn will be able to be ethically responsible when

DOI: 10.4324/9781003315797-12

they meet children and students in a grey zone between the public and the private in preschool or classrooms.

As a teacher educator, I have encountered advantages with online teaching such as having everyone at the same distance and being able to address everyone by name, but also disadvantages in that some remain black boxes and that some lose attention when children or pets show up. A private and professional blur has affected teaching and learning practice environments in different ways. Boundaries between work and private life have been affected and therefore, the period of online teaching and learning has evoked new challenges to protect a private space while continuing to communicate reflectively on personal dispositions, giving space to emotions, self-care, and creating wellbeing. In this chapter, the aim is to discuss how educators can continue to develop reflective learning environments in an ethically responsible manner in the light of conditions formed during the pandemic. Circumstances have forced us to rethink earlier assumptions for better or worse and we need to understand both new challenges and possibilities.

Context

I imagine the shadow in the photo as the preservice teacher acting in a situation, at campus or in school, trying to get a picture of the Self. As an educator, I am either the skier, acting to get the preservice teacher to react and respond or the other shadow, next to the preservice teacher, trying to observe, support, or trigger the reflection. The picture is private and not related to teaching or classrooms showing that reflection on educational matters is not possible to separate from private experiences. Lived experiences shape our life worlds and through reflection, awareness of them can emerge. To support preservice teachers' reflections on themselves, educators must continuously engage in their own self-reflection. When I discuss beliefs, values, and attitudes with preservice teachers, I must balance between the private and the public sphere, between the concrete example and a theoretical understanding as well as between aspects of cognition and emotion.

Opportunities and obstacles with technology

In previous research focusing on reflective learning environments in higher education during the pandemic, both possibilities and obstacles related to technology are discussed. Flexibility is often mentioned but with various meanings. Abas (2021) point to lost flexibility when discussions on zoom automatically end and students are sent back to the main session while discussions in physical meetings are possible to end spontaneously. However, most researchers consider the online teaching as more flexible. Space becomes flexible and when teaching is asynchronous, time becomes flexible (Murray et al., 2020; Zenkov et al., 2021). The advantage of not having to travel is also mentioned in relation to educators' visits when preservice teachers do their internships (Boivin &

Image 9.1 A visual representation of self-awareness through reflection.

Welby, 2021). To McIntosh and Nenonene (2020), flexibility in relation to online teaching instead means offering many and flexible virtual office hours to maintain communication with students. A similar understanding is expressed by Glew et al. (2020) when they discuss how the earlier course might be handled online, balancing between a specific content and the students' needs to discuss and relate to each other. Equity and equality are other aspects discussed in relation to online teaching. Differences in access to networks, computer equipment, and a quiet place to sit affect students' opportunities to assimilate the teaching (Abas, 2021; Ghazi-Saidi et al., 2020; Lei & Medwell, 2021). Murray et al. (2020) identify both difficulties with access to technology and lack of technical competence as obstacles to online teaching. The problem I have experienced in online teaching when students choose to appear like black boxes is also described by Day and Verbiest (2021). The students might have a variety of reasons to turn off their cameras but regardless, a distance arises when you, especially when documents are shared, do not have visible recipients. Bodily expressions are largely lost in Zoom, but if facial expressions and presence are also lost, it becomes difficult to maintain communication and commitment.

Emotions and wellbeing

In times of pandemic, emotions like vulnerability, fear, stress, and anxiety have called for a teaching that clearly involves emotional aspects as well as cognition (Lei & Medwell, 2021; Lemon & McDonough, 2021). To counteract the negative emotions that have arisen in connection with the pandemic, education needs to stimulate and strengthen wellbeing and self-care (Lemon, 2021). The situation during the pandemic has shaken people and self-evident aspects of both life in general and education have to be reimagined (Abas, 2021; Lemon & McDonough, 2021). Educators need to support preservice teachers to confront and deal with emotions like vulnerability and through reflection build their self-awareness and thereby create self-confidence (Lemon, 2021). By stimulating intrinsic motivation, students develop self-confidence and autonomy, which in turn increases wellbeing (Ghazi-Saidi et al., 2020; Joseph & Trinick, 2021; Tymms & Peters, 2020). Wellbeing is a complex concept related to both education and private life and educators sometimes neglect their own self-care (Lemon, 2021). In a study about professional ethics with preservice teachers (Cronqvist, 2015), one of the participants, Emma, is worried about her responsibility in her professional role to take care of herself. She says:

> I want to find a way to actually take care of them [students] and help them in situations, but not in a way that affects myself so that I feel bad because I have to be able to be there, give security to all students and not be at home and feel bad because a student feels bad.
>
> (p. 133)

152   *Marita Cronqvist*

This reflection shows that Emma is aware of the responsibility both towards the students and towards herself and that these responsibilities are related. Another participant in the same study, Eva, expresses how her own wellbeing is related to the students'. When she feels safe, it becomes easier for her to make the students safe (p. 190). Such reflections that often arise in connection with internships have to be captured and discussed in the education. Therefore, the discussion in this chapter about educators' ethical responsibility for reflective teaching in the struggle between the public and the private is needed. The preservice teachers' opportunities to reflect on emotions, self-image, and values in their education influence both their lives in general and their professional role development.

The need for each other

In addition to cognition and emotions as important elements of teaching, attention is also paid to a social dimension (Abas, 2021). Not least in times of pandemic, communication and relationships both between educator-students and between students become urgent to enhance humanity in teaching in spite of physical distance. Glew et al. (2020) share their experiences of opening up meetings on Zoom for students and making it possible for them to meet both with and without the educators' presence. In this way, students can ask educators to discuss certain aspects with them, when and if they want to. The educators argue that they model a flexible view of teaching that preservice teachers might use in their own future teaching. Lei and Medwell (2021) have studied OCL (online collaborative learning) and present several benefits of this model. The collaboration online activates the students and manages to break their feeling of isolation. Their emerging autonomy through the demand to make choices and decisions in the collaboration brings a self-awareness and helps them to formulate their own teaching ideals. In addition, their technical competence seems to be improved overall, which may contribute to them using the technology in future teaching. Cooperative tasks, occasions to share thoughts or reflect together are examples of how an educator in different ways can enhance humanity and wellbeing and break the isolation during a pandemic. Guzy (2020) tells about her decision to let the students watch a program at home and open up an online forum to discuss it. She noticed that this possibility to write comments stimulated the discussion among students who hesitated to comment orally. Another finding was the emotional experience for some of the students to watch the program together with their family. The students' reflections became more personal as the online discussion forum helped them dare to share.

Values and attitudes in an uncertain time

Values such as humanity, safety, and compassion become part of an ethical dimension of teaching that I would like to add in this discussion to visualise and

Ethical responsibility in the struggle between public/private space   153

emphasise the importance of reflections on them. Growing as a person demands courage to share experiences, feelings, and values with other people, which can feel both challenging and uncomfortable (Lemon & McDonough, 2021). Nevertheless, this process, gaining self-awareness and self-confidence, confronting and dealing with values, attitudes, (Cronqvist, 2020) and negative emotions like vulnerability and uncertainty can be an asset in education (Lemon & McDonough, 2021; Murray et al., 2020). As we have seen, online education is not only an obstacle to self-reflection and self-awareness but can support humanity in education. Murray et al. (2020) discuss how the pandemic situation might affect teacher education in a longer perspective. Experiences during a challenging time, globally shared, should not be ignored but used to make sustainable improvements. During the pandemic, people now and then have expressed a wish to go back to what they call normality, as it was before. I argue that it is not possible and perhaps not even desirable to return to previous conditions in life. Experiences continuously change our life worlds, our being to the world (Merleau-Ponty, 2002/1945) and we must make choices and develop ourselves based on new circumstances, in our private lives as well as in teacher education. Advantages experienced from online teaching need to be considered when we make choices between face-to-face and online teaching.

Strategies for responsible reflective learning environment

Ethical leadership in teacher education as well as in preservice teachers' future teaching is based on the values and attitudes that teachers add to teaching. Therefore, awareness of one's own life worlds to understand values and attitudes, must be given attention in the education, which requires educators to dare to enter into the personal, both with themselves and with the preservice teachers. As we have seen in previous research, the transition to online teaching entails both obstacles and benefits for developing preservice teachers' awareness of dispositions as well as their ways to express and process values consciously in teaching. In this tension, I discuss how different strategies for reflective learning environments can be maintained despite the pandemic but also improved through an adaptation to change caused by the pandemic.

Strategy 1

In my lectures, I strive to have a dialogue with the preservice teachers and even though they sometimes are many, I still try to get them to reflect on their positions in different areas. By reading out questions about human and knowledge views, I want to make visible how difficult it is to take a stand and how unconscious we usually are about what values and attitudes we express. Another way to stimulate reflections during lectures is to alternate abstract theoretical aspects with concrete examples that are relevant to preservice teachers' programs. Examples from the lived practice and from experiences expressed by participants in studies might give preservice teachers an opportunity to

154 *Marita Cronqvist*

recognise themselves or gain a better understanding of the theories. In addition, emotions expressed by others can be discussed and become less "dangerous". For example, during internships, less engaged students or students who need more explanations might evoke negative emotions in preservice teachers, which need to be handled so that students do not feel devalued. By giving examples from participants in studies, preservice teachers have the opportunity to discuss without going into the private. In this way, the public and the private are balanced. Preservice teachers are affected but do not have to disclose themselves.

In a lecture hall, preservice teachers can talk in pairs for a couple of minutes to get started with their reflections. On one hand, it is more complicated to enter such quick exchanges in Zoom, but on the other hand, preservice teachers can give examples of their reflections in the chat. This strategy, to offer both oral and written options for comment has been shown to stimulate discussion (Guzy, 2020) and the chat might be complemented with asynchronous discussion forums. Especially if you meet preservice teachers who are black boxes online, different ways of engaging them in questions about values and attitudes need to be tried (Day & Verbiest, 2021). In general, preservice teachers' home environment can both affect them to feel secure and blur the limit to the private. When the family is present, it is closer at hand to give examples and tell about personal experiences (Guzy, 2020). Related to the picture, my role as a lecturer can be compared with the skier, trying to perform something that is inspiring and attracts the participants to reflect on themselves (looking at their shadows), what values they include and act on.

Strategy 2

Reflective teaching to create self-awareness can advantageously be formed in the field between the lived experience during school-based education and the campus-based education. I arrange seminars focusing on dilemmas that preservice teachers have experienced in the encounter with students, colleagues, or parents in school. We usually meet at two occasions when they are back on campus. During the first seminar, the preservice teachers tell about their lived experiences in the individual dilemma one by one and everybody has the opportunity to ask questions, comment, or compare with own experiences. During the second seminar, we discuss the dilemmas related to various ethical models (for example virtue ethics and utilitarianism) and meanings of professional ethics (Cronqvist, 2020). This approach provides a dynamic movement between the concrete subjective perspective and the abstract theoretical perspective. Finally, we compare teachers' professional responsibility in school with the responsibility that researchers have for a study. The last part is difficult for the preservice teachers to relate to but provides additional perspectives on how they experience their professional responsibility and works as a preparation for their final courses in teacher education when they write thesis. This strategy has not been significantly affected during the pandemic. The preservice teachers are happy to share their lived experiences and through meetings in Zoom, it is easy to address them by name and let them tell their stories. Van Manen (2012) points out the importance of using students' names even if one is unsure of the pronunciation. Zoom makes it possible to use the names and thereby, the meeting becomes more personal. Related to the picture, this strategy is about standing behind, listening and supporting as well as stimulating the reflection by asking questions. Sometimes, when preservice teachers find it difficult to relate to theories, my role shifts to the skier's, as I need to give them suggestions and explanations.

Strategy 3

Another strategy to create self-awareness about values and attitudes that takes place in the field between campus- and school-based educations is video paper (Cronqvist, 2019, 2021). The preservice teachers choose film clips from their teaching during school-based education and write reflections on them. Back on campus, they present their clips and reflections in a seminar. Using video is a highly suitable strategy in many aspects during a pandemic. In previous research, videos and case studies (Callaway-Cole & Kimble, 2021; Guzy, 2020) as well as avatars and video recordings (Boivin & Welby, 2021) are studied. Boivin and Welby (2021) point out how video recordings enhance the communication between educators in the field and on campus in supervising preservice teachers' teaching. The gap between theory and practice in teacher education is well known, but in reflective learning, educators can support preservice teachers to interweave their lived practice with theories through different strategies for reflection (Cronqvist, 2019, 2020). The recordings make the preservice teachers nervous (Xiao & Tobin, 2018), which affects their teaching, but when they realise that the nervousness is felt more in the situation than it is visible in recordings and probably in real life, their self-confidence increases (Cronqvist, 2021). However, the educators must ensure that the recordings take place in a learning environment where the preservice teachers feel safe.

I have noticed that educators in the field are more likely to attend joint seminars when arranged via Zoom. The idea existed earlier but the pandemic accelerated the development. Preservice teachers' reflections are stimulated both by observing themselves in recordings and through seminars where educators in the field and at the university with their different competencies meet. One problem with using recordings is the General Data Protection Regulation (GDPR, namely SPS 2018:218), a law concerning EU, which has increased permit requirements. Another problem can be lack of equity concerning access to technology or competence among preservice teachers (Abas, 2021; Ghazi-Saidi et al., 2020; Lei & Medwell, 2021). However, it is worth the effort to overcome the problems because recordings together with the memory image add further dimensions to the reflection (Cronqvist, 2021). Research shows that reflection through video paper is affected by the instructions (Blomberg

156 *Marita Cronqvist*

et al., 2013) and therefore, related to the picture, reflections through video papers demand both the skier to instruct and the shadow next to the preservice teacher to support.

Conclusion

During the pandemic, digitalisation has been forced on society and the previous discussion about advantages and disadvantages is now being replaced by trying to find a balance in teaching based on experiences of what the digital and analogue add in a post-pandemic time. Research indicates a need for attention on humanity, self-care, and wellbeing in higher education and through responsible reflective teaching, self-awareness and self-confidence might emerge in a space between the public and the private in teacher education. Access to technology and technical competence is crucial to equity as well as equality and must be considered in the choice between online and analogue alternatives. The use of video paper and Zoom meetings to improve communication between educators in the field and on campus are elements of strategies where technology is crucial to stimulate reflective teaching. Face-to-face teaching has other benefits such as body language and spontaneous conversations, which must also be taken into account when physical encounters eventually are enabled. Preservice teachers' emotions and wellbeing affect both their professional development as well as their lives in general and they need help to deal with their emotions, both positive and negative, in order to develop a self-care in the professional role that provides sustainability. The isolation that followed in the footsteps of the pandemic has had a major impact on preservice teachers' possibilities to reflect together at physical meetings. Communication via the web has offered opportunities to meet and share thoughts despite the distance. Through synchronous as well as asynchronous forums, written expressions can complement oral, which has been shown to promote reflections. Strategies to stimulate discussions about values and dilemmas create self-awareness and might contribute to preservice teachers' modelling of confidence and safety to future students. A balance between the public and the private, theories and lived practice as well as cognitive and emotional aspects demands an ethical responsibility in the meeting with each preservice teacher. As an educator, I need to both perform and act like the skier in the picture in order to trigger the reflection and inspire the commitment as well as standing behind, like the shadow, observing and being supportive.

References

Abas, S. (2021). Teaching and learning in COVID times: A reflective critique of a pedagogical seminar course. *Journal of Teaching and Learning with Technology*, *10*(1), 34–43. doi:10.14434/jotlt.v9i2.31392

Bates, A. J., Drits, D., & Ramirez, L. A. (2011). Self-awareness and enactment of supervisory stance: Influences on responsiveness toward student teacher learning. *Teacher Education Quarterly*, *38*(3), 69–87.

Blomberg, G., Renkl, A., Sherin, M. G., Borko, H., & Seidel, T. (2013). Five research-based heuristics for using video in pre-service teacher education. *Journal for Educational Research on Line*, 5(1), 90–114.

Boivin, J. A., & Welby, K. (2021). Teaching future educators during a global pandemic. *IAFOR Journal of Education*, 9(2), 25–36.

Callaway-Cole, L., & Kimble, A. (2021). Maintaining professional standards in early childhood teacher preparation: Evaluating adaptations to fieldwork-based experiences during COVID-19. *Early Childhood Education Journal*, 49, 841–853. https://doi.org/10.1007/s10643-021-01227-9

Cronqvist, M. (2015). *Yrkesetik i lärarutbildning – en balanskonst* (Diss.). Göteborgs universitet.

Cronqvist, M. (2019). Reflecting and verbalizing teaching – supported by didactic and digital tools. *Beijing International Review of Education*, 1(2–3), 512–532.

Cronqvist, M. (2020). Professional ethics as experienced by student teachers: A neoliberal view. *Phenomenology & Practice*, 14(1), 89–104.

Cronqvist, M. (2021). Embodied becoming – student teachers' reflections on their filmed teaching. *Video Journal of Education and Pedagogy*, 6(1), 1–16. https://doi.org/10.1163/23644583-bja10017

Dania, A. (2021). An autoethnography of becoming critical in physical education teacher education. *Curriculum Studies in Health and Physical Education*, 12(3), 251–267. doi:10.1080/25742981.2021.1926299

Day, J., & Verbiest, C. (2021). Lights, camera, action? A reflection of utilizing web cameras during synchronous learning in teacher education. *Teacher Educators' Journal*, 14, 3–21.

Egan, H., O'Hara, M., Cook, A., & Mantzios, M. (2021). Mindfulness, self-compassion, resiliency and wellbeing in higher education: A recipe to increase academic performance. *Journal of Further and Higher Education*. doi:10.1080/0309877X.2021.1912306

Farnell, T., Skledar Matijević, A., & Šćukanec Schmidt, N. (2021). *The impact of COVID-19 on higher education: A review of emerging evidence, NESET report*. Publications Office of the European Union. doi:10.2766/069216

Ghazi-Saidi, L., Criffield, A., Kracl, C. L., McKelvey, M., Obasi, S. N., & Vu, P. (2020). Moving from face-to-face to remote instruction in a higher education institution during a pandemic: Multiple case studies. *International Journal of Technology in Education and Science (IJTES)*, 4(4), 370–383.

Glew, S. T., Oto, R., & Mayo, J. B. (2020). With love: Attempting to instill the lasting value of humanity while teaching during a global pandemic. *Journal of International Social Studies*, 10(2), 60–66.

Guzy, A. (2020). Putting the "human" into the humanities. *Journal of the National Collegiate Honors Council*, 21(2), 25–29.

Hagenauer, G., Gläser-Zikuda, M., & Moschner, B. (2018). University students' emotions, life-satisfaction and study commitment: A self-determination theoretical perspective. *Journal of Further and Higher Education*, 42(6), 808–826. doi:10.1080/0309877X.2017.1323189

Joseph, D., & Trinick, R. (2021). 'Staying apart yet keeping together': Challenges and opportunities of teaching during COVID-19 across the Tasman. *New Zealand Journal of Educational Studies*, 56, 209–226. https://doi.org/10.1007/s40841-021-00211-6

Lei, M., & Medwell, J. (2021). Impact of the COVID-19 pandemic on student teachers: How the shift to online collaborative learning affects student teachers' learning and future teaching in a Chinese context. *Asia Pacific Education Review*, 22, 169–179. https://doi.org/10.1007/s12564-021-09686-w

Lemon, N. S. (2021). Wellbeing in initial teacher education: Using poetic representation to examine pre-service teachers' understanding of their self-care needs. *Cultural Studies of Science Education*, 16, 931–950. https://doi.org/10.1007/s11422-021-10034-y

158   *Marita Cronqvist*

Lemon, N. S., & McDonough, S. (2021). If not now, then when? Wellbeing and whole-heartedness in education. *The Educational Forum*, *85*(3), 317–335. doi:10.1080/0013172 5.2021.1912231

McIntosh, N. A., & Nenonene, R. L. (2020). In this spirit: Helping preservice teachers thrive during the pandemic through adaptation and change. *Journal of Catholic Education*, *23*(1), 162–174. http://dx.doi.org/10.15365/joce.2301122020

Merleau-Ponty, M. (2002/1945). *Phenomenology of perception* [Phenomenologie de la perception] (C. Smith, Trans.). Routledge.

Messenger, H. (2015). The identification of a value-based pedagogical pattern promoting development of the person' in higher education. *Teaching in Higher Education*, *20*(7), 738–749. doi:10.1080/13562517.2015.1069267

Murray, C., Heinz, M., Munday, I., Keane, E., Flynn, N., Connolly, C., Hall, T., & Mac-Ruairc, G. (2020). Reconceptualising relatedness in education in 'distanced' times. *European Journal of Teacher Education*, *43*(4), 488–502. doi:10.1080/02619768.2020.1806820

Roland, E., & Jones, A. (2020). Co-teaching difficult subjects: Critical autoethnography and pedagogy. *Teaching in Higher Education*. doi:10.1080/13562517.2020.1839747

Rosengren, P. G. (2009). *Att fånga bildning* (2009:24 R). Högskoleverket.

Schussler, D. L., & Knarr, L. (2013). Building awareness of dispositions: Enhancing moral sensibilities in teaching. *Journal of Moral Education*, *42*(1), 71–87.

Schussler, D. L., Stooksberry, L. M., & Bercaw, L. A. (2010). Understanding teacher candidate dispositions: Reflecting to build self-awareness. *Journal of Teacher Education*, *61*(4), 350–363.

Shapira-Lishinsky, O. (2011). Teachers' critical incidents: Ethical dilemmas in teaching practice. *Teaching and Teacher Education*, *27*(3), 648–656.

Tymms, M., & Peters, J. (2020). Losing oneself: Tutorial innovations aspotential drivers of extrinsic motivation and poor wellbeing in university students. *Pastoral Care in Education*, *38*(1), 42–63. doi:10.1080/02643944.2020.1713871

Tvedt, M. S., Bru, E., & Idsoe, T. (2021). Perceived teacher support and intentions to quit upper secondary school: Direct, and indirect associations via emotional engagement and boredom. *Scandinavian Journal of Educational Research*, *65*(1), 101–122. doi:10.1080/0031 3831.2019.1659401

Van Manen, M. (2012). The call of pedagogy as the call of contact. *Phenomenology & Practice*, *6*(2), 8–34.

Xiao, B., & Tobin, J. (2018). The use of video as a tool for reflection with preservice teachers. *Journal of Early Childhood Teacher Education*, *39*(4), 328–345. doi:10.1080/10901027. 2018.1516705

Zenkov, K., Helmsing, M., Parker, A. K., Glaser, H., & Bean, M. (2021). Portrait of the teacher educator as a weary pedagogue: Narrating our way to a post-pandemic vision of educator preparation. *Teacher Educators' Journal*, *14*, 106–125.

Printed in the USA
CPSIA information can be obtained
at www.ICGtesting.com
LVHW021735041124
795688LV00040B/1262